CREATE YOUR OWN
STAGE LIGHTING

D1417285

CREATE YOUR OWN
STAGE LIGHTING

Tim Streader and John A Williams

A SPECTRUM BOOK

Prentice-Hall, Inc., Englewood Cliffs, New Jersey 07632

Library of Congress Cataloging in Publication Data

Streader, Timothy
Create your own stage lighting

"A Spectrum Book"
Includes index
1. Stage lighting. I. Williams, John (John A.)
II. Title.
PN2091.E4S84 1985 792'.025 85-16728
ISBN O-13-189184-7
ISBN O-13-189176-6 (pbk.)

This book is available at a special discount when ordered in bulk quantities
Contact Prentice-Hall, Inc., General Publishing Division,
Special Sales, Englewood Cliffs, N.J.07632.

Text copyright © Thames Head Limited 1985
Illustration copyright © Thames Head Limited 1985
This design copyright © Thames Head Limited 1985

All rights reserved. No part of this book may be reproduced
in any form or by any means without permission in writing from
the publisher. A Spectrum Book.

First published by Prentice-Hall, Inc., in the USA 1985

1 0 9 8 7 6 5 4 3 2 1

Prentice-Hall International,Inc., *London*
Prentice-Hall of Australia Pty. Limited, *Sydney*
Prentice-Hall Canada Inc., *Toronto*
Prentice-Hall Hispanoamericana, S.A., *Mexico*
Prentice-Hall of India Private Limited, *New Delhi*
Prentice-Hall of Japan, Inc., *Tokyo*
Prentice-Hall of Southeast Asia Pte.Ltd., *Singapore*
Whitehall Books Limited, *Wellington, New Zealand*
Editoria Prentice-Hall do Brasil Ltda., *Rio de Janeiro*

ISBN 0-13-189184-7

ISBN 0-13-189176-6 {PBK.}

While every care has been taken to verify facts and methods
described in this book, neither the publishers nor the authors can
accept liability for any loss or damage howsoever caused. Legal
and safety requirements are subject to change and may vary with
the locality. It is the responsibility of the reader to verify current
regulations.

Typesetting by
Optic, London

Reproduction by
Redsend Limited, Birmingham

Printed in Great Britain by
Purnell & Sons (Book Production) Limited, Paulton

To Margarett Perryman
In memory of her encouragement to me
over the writing of this book (John A Williams)

Create Your Own Stage Lighting was conceived,
edited, and designed by
James Head Limited,
Avening, Tetbury,
Gloucestershire,
Great Britain

Editorial and Marketing director
Martin Marix Evans

Design and Production director
David Playne

Art editor
Barry Chadwick

Editor
Bill Davies

Consultant editor
Professor Robert A. Shakespeare,
Department of Theater and Drama,
Indiana University, Bloomington, Indiana, USA

Designers and illustrators
Heather Church
Terry Thomas
Jacquie Govier
Nick Allen
Tony De Saulles
Nick Hand
David Ganderton
Bob Wood

Other books in this series:

Create Your Own Stage Props
Jacqui Govier
Create Your Own Stage Sets
Terry Thomas
Create Your Own Stage Faces
Douglas Young

Contents

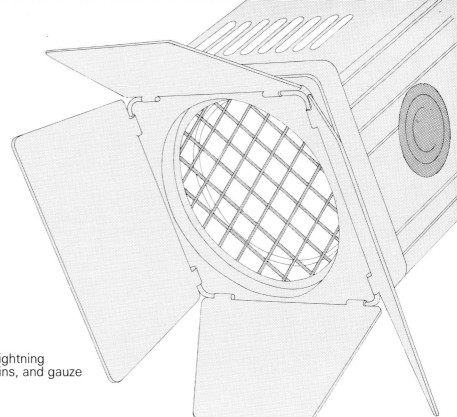

Introduction

In the moments before a play begins, the auditorium is all bustle. Late arrivals apologize as they squeeze their way through to their seats, sweet papers rustle, programs are passed along the row, and general gossip is exchanged. The audience is divided into many separate little groups. Then, suddenly, the lights dim and the last snatches of conversation hush away as the audience becomes as one. The world of make-believe is about to begin, heralded by a change of lighting state.

This is a convention readily accepted. It may, on occasions, be augmented by an orchestral introduction to the evening's entertainment, but it is really this initial darkening of the auditorium that signals to the audience that now they must prepare themselves to become a part of what is to follow. As the lights are then raised on the curtain or stage, all attention is drawn in that direction.

Thus the lighting demonstrates, at the beginning of every performance, that it is a very powerful tool.

Lighting can take many forms and guises. It may be stunning and dramatic, or subtly self-effacing, so that the audience react to its effects while scarcely realizing its presence. Its initial command of audience attention before the curtain is raised may perhaps be divorced from the content of the play itself but, during the rest of the production, the lighting should be an integral part of the drama.

Light can mold the space on the stage with all its architectural characteristics, its color, and its own very elemental dramatic qualities. It is, after all, a form of energy, a basic requirement: light and dark, day and night, black and white — a world of contrasts. Paint the stage with these effectively and the audience will be better able to relate to all the other aspects of production. Moreover, and most important of all, light enables the actor to be seen.

All this can be achieved by technological expertise. It will be necessary to analyze the job in hand, sort out the necessary tools, and then set to work to implement them properly. However, the manipulation of light to create a visual concept is not purely a technical task. It is very much an artistic one and this book sets out to explore both aspects of lighting the stage — the mechanics and the design.

All the basic equipment and the instruments of light are discussed. These include lamps and luminaires, as well as dimmers, control boards, and computer systems. The means to exploit this equipment to the full, by understanding just how a luminaire's position and angle will alter its effect, is also explained; and the electrical principles involved, special effects, and the use of color.

This technical know-how is supplemented by an analysis of production procedure so it can be seen how the lighting plan for any show can be undertaken in a logical and practical fashion, from the first evaluation of the script, through discussion and practical planning, to the final dress rehearsal.

There is much to learn. A brief history of early stage lighting explores the changing fashion in lighting, reflecting both the scientific developments in the world around and the way attitudes to theater and lighting evolved over the years.

The role of the lighting designer can never be divorced from the technicalities of the medium but neither should it ever be totally contained within them. It is a creative art form, and, as such, is a very satisfying element of stage production in which to be involved.

Ideal conditions rarely prevail. This book is not purely for the theorists and so takes into account the fact that resources may be limited and the budget already overstretched. How to cope with limited equipment is fully discussed in one chapter, *Lighting the stage with limited resources,* and is borne in mind throughout the book. Moreover, the fact that anyone new to the field may find it difficult to relate to the subject initially is alleviated by the inclusion of the *Small beginnings* chapter and a comprehensive glossary.

A check should always be made on local regulations and legal requirements so that suitable precautions can be taken and the production will not be marred by any accident or last minute panic to fulfil safety requirements.

Safety is a major consideration. Hazard symbols may be found throughout the book and these indicate where the procedure may be potentially dangerous and caution is required. A chapter on basic electrics

ory and safety serves to
plain in simple terms, the
nciples which are involved
en lighting the stage — but is
y a brief synopsis of these.
this reason, anyone who is
undertake the handling of
ctrical equipment will need a
deeper grasp of the subject
n this chapter can supply.
to be hoped, therefore, that
ch wider reading will
cede practical application of
theories that are discussed.
eral books on the subject
e been included in the
liography.

book recognizes that there
never be a substitute for
l experience, dealing with
particular problems of each
duction, working through
planning stage, setting up
rig, and the rehearsals —
til the moment comes when
lighting is being used in live
eater. Only then can the
ults be properly seen and
aluated. However, it is
ssible through the chapter on
nn A. Williams' own lighting
ductions, to share a little of
experience as a lighting
signer. We can see lighting in
tion, in the real world rather
n the pages of a book, as
ny of the theories are put into
ctice, in live situations in
theater.

is hoped the book will be
aluable in discovering how to
e a wide range of theater
iting and effects, even for the
ginner. At the same time, the
fessional standards of the
thors have been in no way
mpromised through their
ploration of the subject as it
ght be applied to amateur or
ident theater, as well as the
fessional stage.

Many visual elements combine
on the stage to create space
and time and highlight the
action. Lighting is undoubtedly
the most mobile of these. Used
skilfully, it will focus attention,
as required, throughout the
production.

Then, as the curtains close on
the final applause, it will be the
raising of the house lights that
seems to "release" the captive
audience, allowing them once
again to become individuals as
the auditorium fills with light.

◇ Watch out for these
hazard symbols throughout
the book. They will identify
any potentially dangerous
situations!

History of stage lighting

Modern stage lighting has changed dramatically in recent years, with computer control, memory systems, and all that technology has to offer; so much so that the lighting of the previous decade might well seem historical by comparison! It is almost impossible for us to visualize lighting by gaslight or candles a century ago.

There is, however, a great deal to be learned by looking back into the past. An appreciation of how lighting developed will help to underline the principles involved. Understanding how a particular play might have looked when lit by the methods then prevailing could perhaps make for a more sympathetic approach when lighting it today.

It might even be possible to replicate some of the effects.

If nothing else, realizing the problems of the past ought to make us appreciate all the possibilities of today; and the inventiveness and ingenuity of early artists in this field should be an inspiration to every lighting designer!

The earliest forms of theater took place out of doors with the open sky above as the source of light with all its natural random changes of mood and intensity. Presumably the position and design of the structure (when there was one) and the time of day had some bearing on how the light fell, whether shadows were cast, and so on.

Perhaps torches might ha been used for dramatic effec night. Normally, however, audience and actors alike wo have shared the same sky a weather. There would ha been no separation of act and audience by light and d and no dimming of lights announce the start of performance, conventions nowadays take for granted.

A visit to an open performance today may reminiscent of the past but probably regarded as a uniq experience, set apart fr traditional theater.

So how did it all begin? W records remain of the varic steps along the way?

11

The sixteenth century

Stage lighting evolved, as did many technological and artistic advances, with experiments and specialized branches of exploration, some of which can be seen in retrospect as "dead-ends". It grew with the scientific knowledge which fed it, but as it is also an art form, it reflected as well the particular personalities spearheading its evolution.

The history of stage lighting as we know it begins at about this time, when theater had moved indoors and at last some control could be exercised over lighting levels and their effect on the production.

The Italian influence

Leone di Soni, an Italian, stated that a tragedy was best performed in a lower light level than that required by a comedy. Thus the lighting was now obviously being seen as a reflection of the mood of the play being enacted.

At this time, Angelo Ingegneri also suggested that the stage appeared much brighter when contrasted with a darkened auditorium, a fact still exploited today, especially if the available lighting is limited.

In 1539, San Gallo of Florence imitated the sun by filling a crystal sphere with water and lighting it from behind with candles. This sun "rose" at the beginning of the play, moved across the "sky" and then "set" as the action closed.

Moons were represented in a similar way, while lightning consisted of pieces of jagged-shaped wood covered in tinsel and flown across on wires!

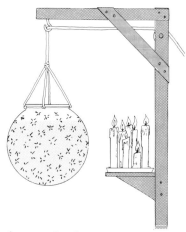

A crystal sphere

Liquid tinting existed at this time but was found to reduce the light's intensity so it was conserved for such special effects as jeweled windows and festive lights on buildings. Thus the lighting designer's golden rule held true even then: The main function of the lighting was to illuminate the actor. In fact the Renaissance artists at this time began to formulate many of the artistic principles which are still valid today.

Lighting and scenic effects

In 1545, yet another Ital Sebastiano Serlio, develo the use of lighting with scen The actual lighting emana from a single chande centrally positioned, but scenic views were desig and painted to look as thou they were lit from one side o

Roundels and windows w made of transparent mater with lights placed behind. Gl containers which held colo water, or sometimes e wine, were fastened on battens and used to ref different tints. Stage thun and lightning was effecti created and "heavenly bod flew through the air by means of wire and thread!

In 1585, Scamozzi placed lig at the side of his scenery, wh was found to be far m effective than existing forms lighting. This idea was taken by Inigo Jones, who introdu it into the English theater.

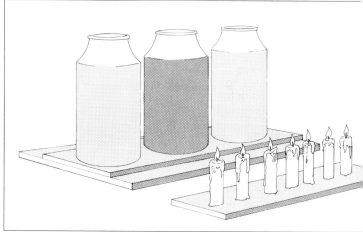

Colored liquids in glass containers reflected different tints

The seventeenth century

1665, Sabbattini developed the concept of lighting from the side. He demonstrated that lighting from one side had a far more pleasing effect that when the stage was lit from the front.

fact, the Renaissance artists developed and mastered most the lighting techniques which continued to be used until the eighteenth century.

The masque

was now that the masque became fashionable, with great expense lavished on effects which became ever more extravagant and spectacular. Through this medium, the first really unified "scenographic" picture appeared on the English stage in *The Masque of Blackness* when motion, light, and costume all contributed to the dramatic effect.

single stage set incorporated moving sea with breaking waves created by perspective illusion. No less than twelve separate masques appeared on this ocean, set in a huge shell and accompanied by moving sea-horses, mermaids, and sea monsters. These were all illumined by a chevron of lights which also rocked on the ocean waves, while twelve torch bearers directed extra light on the rich silk of the costumes.

et above this heaving ocean was a cloudy night sky, from which a personified moon was later to appear, dressed in white and silver, sitting on a throne, and crowned with a sphere of light which was to illumine all the clouds. The heavens were vaulted with blue silk and studded with silver stars.

This, no doubt, all seems too rich to our modern taste, going "over the top" with a vengeance! However, it must certainly have made quite an impression on the audience at the time, and was an explosion of new ideas, a journey of discovery into all that could be theatrically achieved.

Oil lamps and candlelight

It comes as quite a shock to realize that all these lighting effects discussed so far were being achieved by candle power and oil lamps. Candles were prefered in the auditorium as oil lamps produced too much smoke and smell, and even these needed trimming every twenty minutes or so.

There was usually only one chandelier placed over the forestage to light both this and the auditorium. Down-stage lighting was provided by footlights, which were mounted behind a parapet set a short distance in front of the stage. Perhaps the mystical effect of some of the scenes was helped by the misty haze of smoke all these lights produced!

On the stage the lights were concealed from view (masked). Behind the proscenium and the wings were placed vertical poles supporting several oil lamps set in evenly spaced rings (the forerunner of modern "lighting trees" or "booms"!)

Other lamps were mounted on horizontal battens at the back of the front valance and the borders. Tinsel, mica, and even polished copper basins were used to make reflectors to increase the efficiency of these early lamps.

The seventeenth century

Darkening the stage

Next time you watch the lights slowly fade out on a scene, imagine how difficult it must have been in the past to darken the stage. There were three possible methods:

First, the lights were simply extinguished. This could be very inconvenient if the stage needed to appear brightly lit again, a few moments later.

A better method was to suspend open cylinders over the candles. These cylinders could then be raised or lowered as necessary.

Third, the lamps could be mounted on rotating poles which were able to swivel away from or toward the area of stage concerned.

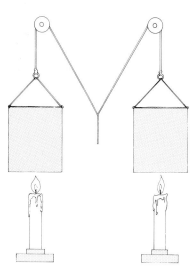

Lighting takes many forms

When an exceptionally bright light was required, these were often concealed in a specially designed scenic device. Yet another grotto, shell, or cloud would be placed conveniently near the object or performer who was to benefit from the extra light. These trappings all incorporated a downstage rim to hide the lamps.

Footlights were now being used in England, largely because of the necessity to fully appreciate the dancers' legs! Fire was also a major problem, with all these open flames exposed. Oil wicks were often floated on water or oil vats to alleviate the risk — hence the term "floats".

The year 1610 saw one of the first performances enacted at night. Hitherto any productions that continued into the late afternoon merely used the light still available through the windows and a chandelier or two. It is worth noting that this is another convention we may take for granted. Theater has only comparatively recently been a creature of the night!

Most performances had to be daytime activities because of the lighting difficulties. The length of time available for a performance was not restricted to the shorter evening period and many lasted for five or six hours or more, with lunch being consumed during the course of the play. This is why so many old plays require drastic cutting to fit into today's evening niche.

Samuel Pepys attended some evening performances and he noted in his diary that the actresses made quite a show by candlelight! He also commented, with considerably less enthusiasm, that the candlelight caused headaches!

Lighting was also used at th time as a diversion from sce changing in the interval. Tethys Festival, music was us to smother the noise of t machinery involved when t audience was entertained between the scene changes, three revolving circles of lig and glass descending befc their eyes.

By 1640 masques we becoming less popular. T exploration of motion and lig had reached its zenith in t myriad candles and color lamps, the exotic scenery, a baroque costumes.

England was being compar unfavorably with France a Italy for not yet knowing how position lights to their be advantage. There were ma quarrels over the complex, a very cumbersome machine required for these spectacu productions, so much so th one producer reverted to simplistic production, using ju one light center stage.

In 1674 a production of T *Tempest* at the Dorset Gard Theater used, for the first tim the dimming of lights. As t ship sank all the house ligh were slowly dimmed and shower of fire fell. This w achieved by raising t chandelier and lowering t footlights, while shields we dropped over the wing lights

In general, the auditorium s remained lit. The glorious por of the masque was s sometimes reflected in t grand finale of a play, w transparent silk backcloths from behind to reveal scenes heaven and deities.

The eighteenth century

ring this period light gradually came far more controlled. The lights placed on vertical sliders behind the wings were able to be dimmed by "scene hands" and footlights were mounted on pivots so they too could be more easily lowered when dimming.

Henry Angelo

Henry Angelo visualized his scenes as transparencies. He advocated far greater subtlety scenic design, and to help achieve this, he introduced transparent backcloths behind which visionary figures could be glimpsed. Color was more carefully controlled too by means of silk screens of scarlet, crimson, and blue. By placing a powerful light in front of these and then turning them towards the scenes, their colors could be reflected in turn so that the stage appeared to be on fire.

David Garrick

In 1765 David Garrick reputedly introduced many new lighting techniques, though it is unclear today which reforms can actually be credited to him. We know that hoops of candles, indiscriminately hung over the stage so that they covered buildings and landscapes, were replaced after his tour abroad. Instead he installed a new type batten incorporating lamps and reflectors which could be swivelled, so that different degrees of light could be obtained according to the time day required.

Philip de Louterbourg

French scene designer, Philip de Louterbourg, was engaged by David Garrick in 1771. His improvements at Drury Lane introduced higher lighting costs. They rose from about £340 per annum to around £1970. His ideas were based on the Italian Renaissance and he favored wild landscapes, picturesque effects, and strong dramatic lighting. He also believed the English temperament "nurtured on mists and nuances of light" would appreciate the less formal and more romantic approach. He became a pioneer in this field and took complete control of the visual side of production in a way that had not occurred since Inigo Jones.

The theater's lighting system, scene shifting, costumes, scenery, machinery, and decor were all to contribute to this unified picture and had to be adapted accordingly.

The range of lighting effects was expanded and far more subtle transitions were made possible. The use of transparent colored silks to reflect light on to the scenes was developed so that a "vast body and brilliancy of colour" could be readily used "with enchanting effect". For instance, a forest scene could suddenly change from green to blood red (a transition which was pronounced "garish" by Gainsborough).

At last machinery miracles had disappeared. Truth to nature became the ultimate aim. Philip de Louterbourg was described as "The first artist who showed that by a just disposition of light and shade....and perspective, the eye of the spectator might be so effectively deceived.... as to take the produce of art for real nature".

By 1781 oil lighting was improved by cylindrical wicks and glass chimneys which made the light steadier and much brighter. Moreover the chimneys could be colored, which simplified these effects. The improvements in lighting enabled actors to move further behind the proscenium arch.

Oil lamp with glass chimney

De Louterbourg demonstrated the effects of this improved light in his model theater. The passing of opaque or colored materials in front of illuminated semi and fully transparent surfaces was greatly admired when it took the form of the sun and moon reflected on water. By 1785 De Louterbourg, and some ballet companies, were exploring the use of gauzes.

Panoramas and dioramas

It was now that panoramas began to appear, first seen in Edinburgh and mostly used for pantomime, as were the first dioramas. This innovation consisted of partly transparent scenery, which remained stationary while screens and shutters manipulated natural light to give a variety of effects.

The nineteenth century

The arrival of gas lighting

The beginning of this century saw dramatic changes with the introduction of gas lighting. In 1822, the New Opera in Paris opened with all the latest developments, including gas lights and a water system to create waterfalls and fountains.

Gas light had in fact first been used on stage in Philadelphia in 1816 and it reached Covent Garden and Drury Lane a year later. There was as yet no gas-mains system, so each theater had to provide its own independent supply and its own maintenance.

Despite the oppressive heat and fumes the gas produced, its remarkable effects were soon fully appreciated. The sudden appearance of the lights from out of the gloom was seen as the striking of daylight, white, regular, and pervading. For the first time every part of the stage could be seen with equal clarity. Its greater flexibility and its intensity made possible many transitions, such as the sun setting, twilight pervading the sky, or a starlit night glimmering above the sea. Many new possibilities opened up, and the invention of mirror flats to reflect the light added to the range of effects.

By 1843 gas was installed at the Comedie-Française in Paris but the actresses complained that the new light was rather too harsh, so the footlights here remained as oil lamps. In some theaters, footlights developed into a large cluster, "the rose", to which actors had to move if making an important speech.

Limelight and the carbon arc

Limelight was used in Covent Garden in the 1830s to add to the brilliance of dioramas of Italian and Alpine scenery. However it was found to be rather expensive and was not used again until 1851.

By the 1840s, theaters in France were also experimenting with limelight, which had been invented in 1816 by Thomas Drummond, an Englishman. Two cylinders of compressed gas (one of hydrogen and one of oxygen) were directed against a column of lime, which was then heated to produce a great incandescence.

In 1846, a carbon arc (first demonstrated by Sir Humphry Davy in 1808) was used at the Opera to create a rising sun effect. It was rather a harsh, flickering light and somewhat noisy. The system was much improved in 1876 with the invention of the Jablochkov Candle by a young Russian engineer living in Paris.

New inventions and improvements

In England, gas was becoming ever more available and widely adopted. There was a new-found sense of freedom now that there were no wicks to trim or candles to replace. Gas lights could be better positioned and so border lights became more popular. The invention of the fishtail burner in 1850 lessened the fumes and made the system all the more efficient, as did the introduction of the "Gas-Table" (the equivalent of today's Gas Board).

At last the gradual dimming house lights could be read effected. By 1849 the curtain darkness had dropped betwe the spectator and the stage.

The greater flexibility of lig helped the development transformation scenes us painted gauzes. Scenes we apparently magically revea and then rendered invisi once again.

Limelight was again introduc and its mellow, brilliant rays le themselves to atmosphe scenes and moonlight, but it s required constant supervisio

All these new lighting system made dramatic differences stage lighting, both in Euro and America, but artis principles were still sa lacking. Moreover the light was as yet only gene illumination, without any of t spotlights that are now familiar to us. In 1860, howev a hood and lens was added the carbon arc to create the ve first spotlight.

During the 1860s, Char Fechter, manager of t Lyceum, introduced an ea prototype of the cyclorama. was really an overhead sl cloth which "mingled softly w the horizon". He also organiz a system of gas footligh below the sloping level of t stage, so arranged that t whole float could be sunk a its red or green lights turned instantaneously or gradually, appropriate.

Sir Henry Irving

In 1878 Sir Henry Irving to over the management of t

he twentieth century

:eum. He was really the first tish producer to make an art stage lighting and to analyze d supervise its use in a :ailed fashion.

 first innovation was to split the footlights and borders different sections with parate colors and controls. also experimented with nsparent lacquered glass, spite criticism that this made lighting arbitrary and tracting. In order to prevent iting spill, Irving introduced use of black masking pieces the front of the stage.

irty gas men were needed to unt and operate all the lights :he Lyceum as the auditorium s, for the first time, nsistently darkened during performance.

ie arrival of electricity

e incandescent gas mantle d by now made the lighting en safer, but at the end of the ntury, electricity began to place it. The potential of ison's discoveries were mediately exploited by the eaters of the world. There ire those, however, who efered the richer, more nospheric gaslight, including Henry Irving.

1881 Richard D'Oyly Carte ened up his new theater in ndon, the Savoy, with Gilbert d Sullivan's *Patience*. This is the first time in London that play was lit throughout with e new electricity.

r Hubert von Herkomer

a little theater in Bushey, irkomer was experimenting

further with the use of gauze and backcloths. His cloud effects were so convincing that the audience had to be shown that this was only an illusion. He was one of the first to abolish footlights because their light was so unnatural, and to see the possibilities of projection, using a magic lantern to create his moving clouds.

Herkomer developed many of our modern principles. He showed that inexpensive materials, if properly lit, could be more effective than skilfully painted silks. He strove to achieve a total work of art, insisting that "it is through the management of light that we touch the real magic of art".

This was echoed in a production of *Faust* in 1886, when color and movement were harmonized, Mephistopheles' scarlet cloak echoing the sunset, and the lighting producing both warm sunshine and cooler brown and gray shades — a far more naturalistic approach.

By this time nearly all English theaters were using electric lighting, although the low wattage then provided meant that carbon arc and limelight were still quite important elements of the lighting, and remained so until after the First World War.

Before very long, significant improvements in the design of lamp filaments made higher wattages possible, and by 1913 1kw lamps were available in Europe. Spotlights were becoming far more popular, and those mounted in the auditorium gradually replaced the footlights. There was much

experimentation at this time with new lighting positions and bridges and the use of color.

Adolphe Appia

Adolphe Appia, a Swiss-born German, was the man who probably had the greatest influence on stage lighting and scenic design at the turn of the century. Initially his ideas were denounced as impractical but in actual fact they had an enormous impact, both on practical applications of the new technology and on the whole approach to lighting.

He was one of the first designers to see the real possibilities of electric light, how it could be used to show the ever-changing quality of natural light, and its diffusion and movement. Up to this time, stage lighting had always been inexorably static.

He was also very interested in using 3-D to create far more realistic sets. He employed light to accentuate the solidity of structures by creating a strong contrast between the highlights and the shadows.

Appia had worked with Wagner and applied his precept of trying to establish a unity between all the various theater arts. He saw light as the most important element in fusing these creative forces. Appia dreamed of manipulating and orchestrating light, like a musical score!

Previously lighting had been simple, crude, and clumsy to operate, so it was usually only raised and lowered at the beginning and the end of a play. This was now all to change.

The twentieth century

The plasticity of light and its direction were to be controlled at last. Sets were more realistic and the lighting changes became unobtrusive; no longer dramatic transitions "before your very eyes".

Appia argued that the director should control all elements of production and that the lighting was primarily for the actor, not the scenery. (In the United States, the scenic designer was actually responsible for the lighting.) Appia's reforms led to mobile overhead illumination which could help mold the gestures of the actors and highlight the patterns and shapes of the groups on the stage. Light should not be squandered on the superficial.

With better color projection, painted colors became less important. The invention of an arc lamp which could be used for indirect illumination and diffusion helped in the realization of all these ideas, and Appia's theories spread throughout Europe.

Edward Gordon Craig

Edward Gordon Craig, who was an English contemporary of Appia's, was greatly influenced by him and especially admired his ideas on spatial abstraction. Craig was also regarded as an impractical theorist, especially as he took Appia's ideas one stage further and insisted on director control. He really would have liked to dispense with actors altogether and convey the action by scenery, dance, movement, and light. Perhaps even the play itself was superfluous! Everything could be reduced to its essential elements. He even suggested staging *Macbeth* in two colors only, brown for the man and gray for the mist.

Craig also further developed Herkomer's gauze device. He added lighting from above to give greater depth of color. Gelatines of blue, amber, and green lit a backcloth which was gray or ultramarine, depending on the mood of the opera. Then, in 1902, he replaced the painted backcloth with a simpler one which consisted of graduated colors, from white at the base to indigo at the top.

The German influence

At about the same time, German innovators were further developing the use of the cyclorama. Either a backing was stretched over vertical rollers or it was dome shaped to partially cover the stage and prevent awkward edges being visible. In England, Reinhardt adapted the flat version with curved ends and used it as a light reflector. Bands of colored silk travelled on rollers and reflected luminous soft tints on to the neutral cyclorama. This was a far more gentle and subtle affect than direct lighting on a painted backcloth.

During the 1920s there was something of a battle between the German lighting system of localized spotlighting and the compartment batten, made popular in Britain by Samoiloff. It provided mainly all-over floodlighting and color effects, and was also being used in the United States. In general, there were four main steps forward; the more efficient lamp, a better reflector, improvement in color techniques, and a shift theater convention wh began to emphasize select control of the stage picture.

By now light was much bright With each new source of lig from candles and oil, through gas and electricity, and th the more powerful reflec battens. The increase in lig intensity was significant, ev dramatic in some cases, but today's standards, it would s seem comparatively dark!

In 1933 aluminum scene which would catch the lig was introduced by Theodc Komisarjevsky. His *King L* made a great impression. It w performed on a spacious, ba stepped stage, the action taki place in pools of light whi flowed, swirled, and chang in color.

Harold Ridge installed wh was then one of the fine lighting systems in the world the Cambridge Festi Theatre. He was a disciple Appia and implemented ma of his ideas. Settings a costumes were illuminat with moving symbolic col Light was the predomina factor, used to suggest with the hollow box of the stage the form, color, and symbolis that Appia had dreamed abo

Front projection was used mc dramatically on the cyclorama *The Hairy Ape*, when t struggle of the gorilla w projected in gigantic shadow and in 1931 Harold Shor production of *Waltzes frc Vienna* at the Alhambra us great batteries of spotlights supplement the normal batte and footlights.

the United States, the use
the profile spot dates
n about this time, being
oduced on a large scale.
ish lamp manufacturers
re unable to make a suitable
p for almost thirty years,
the difference in voltages
vented their importation.

phasis on the visual creation
ght continued to occupy the
ting designer's imagination
ughout the next twenty
rs or so. Not all of the
erimentation was wholly
ctical. In some cases, the
ovation shocked audiences.
roduction of *Tannhauser* in
4, which used light and
jection instead of scenery,
sed quite an outrage.

956 Brecht encouraged the
of projected photographs
moving pictures. The
act of slides and films could
quite stunning (as seen later
Oh What a Lovely War!).
cht also advocated the use
tark white light.

ing the post-war years, the
erican musical made an
ortant impression on the
ld of theater. When
ahoma was first produced,
nveiled a totally different
erience in choreography and
ging. This led to the
tinuing influence of "The Big
sical" with all its color and
sh production techniques.

dern lighting equipment was
readily available, with most
the luminaires and dimmers
iliar today. These have
iously been improved and
ned. The age of the
nputer has accelerated this
tinuous pattern of finer
hnology and ease of control.

The creative element

It is still the ideas and the
application of the lighting
designer's vision that enables
all these different pieces of
equipment to be so effective.

Today designers, such as Ralph
Koltai, are exploring the use of
plastics because of the great
light quality that these contain.
His abstract designs have
transferred to the stage the
optical and illusory effects of
modern art.

We have come a long way from
crystal spheres lit by candles,
and even further from the open
sky. Lighting effects have
swung from the ostentatious

heavenly vistas used in the
seventeenth century to the
close imitation of nature, and
then to symbolic pools of color.
Sometimes a new invention has
spearheaded new ideas, and
sometimes the ideas have
sought out the practical means
to make them possible.

Just what the future holds
cannot be predicted. The past
can be seen as a carousel of
many different techniques and
fashions, but throughout it is the
role of the lighting designer that
has grown consistently. It is the
way the available lighting has
been exploited and its visual
impact on the stage that has
helped each era to achieve its
own particular magic.

The role of a lighting designer

What is a lighting designer? Such a person did not exist in the days of Greek drama and does not exist today in open street theater. So what exactly happens when theater moves indoors? How does lighting contribute to a play, and what is the role of the lighting designer? It would be more accurate, in fact to ask, "What roles?" because there are many.

The lighting designer will soon find that the role extends far beyond simple illumination of the stage. He or she is a working member of a team, whose overall aim is to achieve a successful and co-ordinated theatrical production. So, when all is not well with other aspects of the production, the lighting designer may find himself coming to the rescue and trying to adapt the lighting to help a fellow member of the production team.

For instance, the designer may be asked, "Can you light out those wrinkles?" when a stage cloth has been badly hung or creased; or a set designer may say, "I haven't achieved quite the right color on that wall; can you light a little more blue into it?" Next might come the director's admission, "I have blocked that little scene rather badly over there; can you divert the emphasis to the group stage left?"

So what roles should the lighting designer expect to play?

The creative role

Design and illumination

First and foremost, a lighting designer should be an artist, not a lighting mechanic or someone who has just "come to do the lights". Most people with a fairly basic knowledge of stage lighting should be able to illuminate an acting area. To add a design quality to this basic lighting lifts that person into a different category. He or she becomes a lighting designer.

Lighting the actor

It is still true to say that the main function of the lighting designer, before attempting any special effects or innovations, is to light the stage so that the actor can be seen. It is totally useless to have a beautifully illuminated stage and set, if the acting area is so badly lit that the actors' faces are hidden in shadow.

So, first and foremost, do remember the golden rule: light the stage so that the actors can be seen.

It has been said that an actor who cannot be seen, cannot be heard. There is definitely a close relationship between the two senses. In any event, actors need to be audible and visible, and it is the lighting designer's first task to see to the latter requirement.

Lighting the stage

Having achieved this basic illumination of the actor, the designer should then light the stage in a way that will be creative, enhancing both the set and the costumes, as well as highlighting the drama. It should never, in any way, detract from these other aspects of the production. A good lighting designer will plan to add mood and atmosphere to the piece, but still keep all the above requirements in mind while doing so.

Special effects

The lighting designer is often called upon to create special effects. Depending on the organization of each individual theater, these effects may not be restricted to lighting effects. They may be any effect that is electrical — or powered by electrical means — such as smoke, dry-ice, pyrotechnics (bangs and flashes), and all the electrical props.

The production team

Throughout all this, the lighting designer should also be aware of the set designer's problems, particularly that of "masking" ; that is the way the set can both hide (and sometimes obstruct) all the mechanics of a play, including all the equipment the lighting necessarily requires.

Consultation with a lighting designer early in the planning stage could solve difficulties that might otherwise become major problems in the later development of the play.

It is obviously beneficial to both parties if the lighting designer can work closely with the set designer to achieve a mutually compatible visual concept.

This is particularly important when certain parts of a set require lighting to make them work — such as backlit cloths or gauze transformations.

The script

In these early stages, it always a bonus if a lightir designer extracts informatic from the script, over and abov the more obvious requiremen dictated by the time of day or t the switching on and off lights. There is often far more be discovered on a clos investigation of the playscrip So it can be seen that a lightir designer can contribute a gre deal to the conception of production — even befo seeing the set or costum designs. He or she should nev be just a puppet who illuminate only other people's idea Otherwise the role will revert that of an illuminator, a opposed to a lighting designe

Awareness and observation

Like many other artists designers, a lighting design can, of course, borrow develop further other people ideas. Do not be too insula Visits to libraries, art gallerie and so on (perhaps in order research visual aids) can ofte spark off an idea. So, of cours can nature itself. The variou qualities of simple daylight are kaleidoscope of many differe colors, changing moods ar atmospheres. Nature achieve unwittingly all the lightin "structures" we shall stud later, from side light at ear morning sunrise, moving c through every angle up to top back light at noon, and the returning to side light at dusk. doing so, it can produce an arra of vivid colors we woul scarcely dare reproduce c stage but which are quit natural out of doors.

adow cast by a tree when sun is overhead

eflection of the sun on water

Pattern of shadows cast by a fence

ngled shadows as the sun moves round

The organizing role

Management and mechanics

Lighting designers will need to be competent managers; they must organize people and production scheduling, and allocate time accordingly.

When the designer is "on-site", the achievement of the final design in the time allowed is very much a team effort.

For instance, the lighting crew may well have worked all through the previous night — or even have spent several days constructing the lighting "rig". Now an arduous focusing session lies ahead of them.

At this point, the lighting designer arrives, probably feeling full of enthusiasm and certainly far more wide-awake than the crew. It is as well to remember the many hours of work already undertaken by the crew. Respect and appreciation of their efforts at this time will result in mutual co-operation. A jammed shutter might be released in seconds, or take many precious minutes to free if the crew is disgruntled!

Ideally, the lighting designer should be capable of estimating the time required for the crew to rig; and how much time he or she needs to focus and light.

Allow about three minutes to focus each luminaire. In actual fact, most of them will take less than two minutes, although sometimes the inaccessability of a luminaire may lengthen the focusing session.

Sometimes, for example, lamps over a set can be reached only by the painstaking manipulation of ladders or Tallescopes" (used when it is necessary to focus by estimation).

"Bouncing bars" (or light pipes) may have to be used. The lighting bar is lowered to a reachable position, the focus estimated, and the luminaire then returned to its "dead" (the final hanging position). This process may have to be repeated several times before the focus is correct.

Experience will give the lighting designer a better grasp of time estimation. Meanwhile, it is preferable to over-estimate. It is much better to have a pat on the back for finishing a couple of hours early than having to contend with bad feeling because the work takes two hours longer than scheduled.

Any stress or frustration will be most unwelcome at the next stage — the lighting session. This takes place at the end of the "fit-up", when the lights are rigged and focused and the set is up and working.

The last thing a lighting designer wants is pressure to finish during the lighting session as it is at this stage that the designer's final visual concept is realized.

Sometimes, however, the set may not be ready on time and this is often a frustrating delay for the lighting team.

Hopefully, all will be well. The set is up and functioning and the focusing is complete. The lighting crew have not turned hostile, and, despite all the pressures, team spirit prevails!

The lighting designer ha succeeded in his role as manager. Now it is possible revert once more to the role an artist, a creator of tim space, and atmosphere, through the medium of light.

Aims

To be a designer, not just a illuminator

To light the stage so that th actors can be seen

To analyze the script careful and fulfil all its dictates

To work well as a member the production team and c operate with the others at th planning stage, giving practic help to alleviate any lat problems that arise

To enhance both the set ar the costumes

To be creative, using light to the stage with mood ar atmosphere

To be able to provide th appropriate special effects

To be a good manager of peop and time

To be inventive

In order to achieve these aim try to be receptive to new idea and do not be afraid experiment. Be aware of lig in the world around, of all i illuminating qualities.

Research as widely as possib and make good use of practic experience. Always try to wor closely with the productic team and with the director.

The lighting designer's role

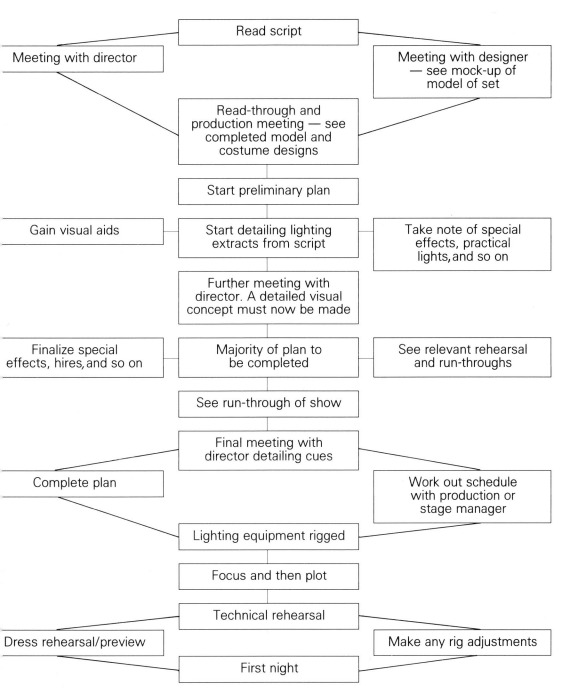

Read script

Meeting with director

Meeting with designer — see mock-up of model of set

Read-through and production meeting — see completed model and costume designs

Start preliminary plan

Gain visual aids

Start detailing lighting extracts from script

Take note of special effects, practical lights, and so on

Further meeting with director. A detailed visual concept must now be made

Finalize special effects, hires, and so on

Majority of plan to be completed

See relevant rehearsal and run-throughs

See run-through of show

Final meeting with director detailing cues

Complete plan

Work out schedule with production or stage manager

Lighting equipment rigged

Focus and then plot

Technical rehearsal

Dress rehearsal/preview

Make any rig adjustments

First night

Equipment and basic techniques

In order to fulfil all the roles of the lighting designer, a thorough understanding is needed of all the equipment available and the necessary lighting techniques that can be used. The lighting designer can then light the actor and the stage, using design and illumination in a creative way.

It is therefore important to be familiar with the functions and particular merits of each piece of equipment that is likely to be within the experience of the designer concerned. This will obviously vary according to the size and budget of the theater or group concerned.

This chapter describes various luminaires that are available for theatrical use, their particular merits, their disadvantages, and how to focus and maintain them. Patching boards and control boards (both manual and computerized memory systems), along with lamps and dimmers, are discussed in sufficient detail to enable even a complete novice to appreciate their individual attributes and application.

The designer must then exploit this equipment to the full, and this can be achieved only by understanding the basic principles of lighting technique.

Front light, side light, back light, down light, up light, and silhouette; all these different ways of lighting the actor and the stage are fully explored, well as the meaning of key a fill light. All this knowledge m be absorbed and put i practice before the desig can become truly expert.

Moreover it will be very diffic to communicate with the res the production team with this basic know-how. It pointless to demand impossible of electricia control-board operators, or equipment itself. At the sa time, one's "vision" should be cramped by technicalities

Try to understand fully wha involved and then find means to achieve y perception of the play, desp any limitations imposed.

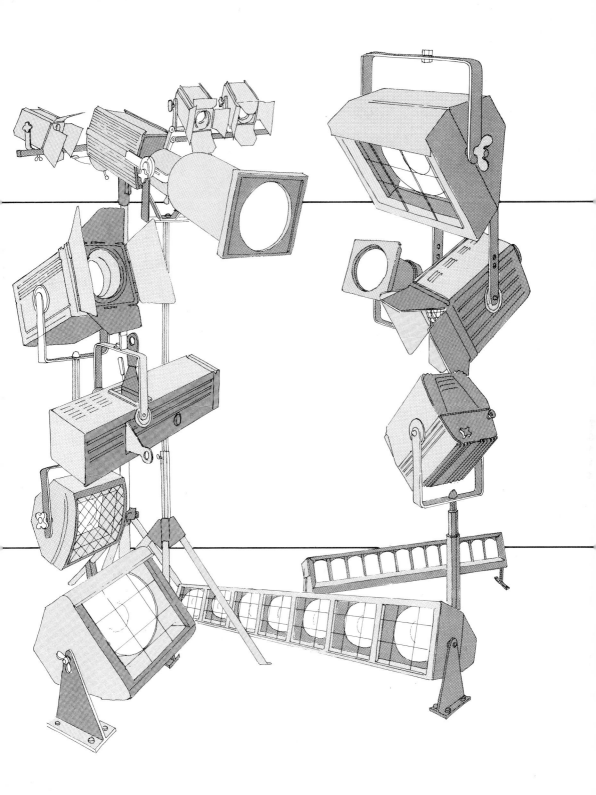

Luminaires

The range of lighting and equipment available for the theater today is enormous, and growing larger all the time, as new technology introduces new equipment.

Just a glimpse at the vast array of luminaires (or instruments) in a professional theater (or the number of pieces of equipment on a lighting plan) can be a daunting experience for the uninitiated.

However, there are many variations on a theme; it is really not as complex as it first appears. Basically, only five types of luminaire are regularly used and these are:

The Profile spot
The Fresnel spot
The Pebble-convex luminaire
The Par
The Flood

A beam light or projector, which is rather like a modified searchlight, might also be used.

The term luminaire merely means any lamp fitted within a casing — as opposed to a naked lamp. Within each type of luminaire, up to four wattage sizes are available, these normally being 500 watt, 750 watt, 1000 watt, and 2000 watt.

Choosing the right wattage size is very important, especially to the amateur, for two reasons.

The first, and most important factor to consider, is the number of luminaires that can be used with the available mains supply.

For instance, it is obviously possible to use twice as many 500 watt luminaires than 1000

watt luminaires on the same mains supply. So, if a large number of lights are required, this might be the better option.

Whichever lights are chosen, it is essential to know all the limitations of the electrical supply and to always keep well within them. (See page 155.)

The second factor to consider is the relationship between the audience and the stage. In a theater where the audience is seated close to the stage, less light will be needed to reflect off the stage area than when the audience are farther away.

Having considered all particular requirements of play, as well as the limitation: the electrical supply and proximity of the audience, n the attributes of all the differ luminaires can be considere

The profile spot
ellipsoidal reflector spotlig

The profile spot provides a ha edged beam of light. This be is of a fixed size, is very inten and has minimum flare (or st light) outside the beam. A: general rule, the narrower beam angle, the greater intensity of light produced.

1 Shutters
2 Plano-convex lens
3 Lens (tube) focus knob
4 Color-frame runners (holders)
5 Gate, with slot for irises and gobos
6 Flat-field/peak knob (lamp alignment)
7 Lamp and ellipsoidal reflector housing

is is achieved because the otlight has a gate aperture ced between the light source d the lens.

e maximum amount of light ailable is collected from the np by the reflector and is then ssed through the gate. This te, and its built-in shutters, termine the profile of the am. The light is then focused a plano-convex lens (a lens ich is flat on one side and sed on the other, as opposed a convex lens).

ur separate shutters are built o the gate to allow shaping of e beam. Some profiles have extra set of shutters, which mounted away from the te to provide a soft, out-of-cus beam.

te runners allow for the sertion of irises. These will ry the size of the circular ttern of light (like the f. stop of camera).

ernatively, a gobo (or cookie) n be inserted. This is a special t-out slide or template which ates a pattern of shadows. It very useful for creating eresting effects, such as ken light dappling through ves, or rippling water.

e way light fills a beam can o be altered and this is called t field or peak, respectively.

t field means that the light is read evenly throughout the am. Peak means that a larger ount of light is concentrated the center of the beam.

me profiles are designed to vide a beam of variable size. ese luminaires have two lenses which can move independently of each other. One lens is used to vary the size of the beam; the other lens adjusts the focus.

The profile spot is a very useful piece of equipment because it is particularly efficient.

Focusing profiles

The hard or soft edge of the beam can be focused by the movement of the lens (diagram 1 and 2). The beam size can be adjusted when the luminaire is one which provides a variable beam.

Vary the beam size with an iris to make it smaller. Shape the beam with shutters to create both hard and soft focus (diagram 3).

Use a gobo (or cookie) for texturing or for projecting an image (diagram 4).

The distribution of light across a beam can be altered. This is called peak or flat field adjustment.

1 A hard-edged beam

2 A soft-edged beam

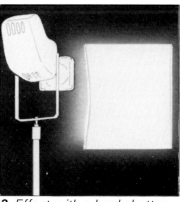

3 Effect with a hard shutter used on the right, and a soft shutter on the left

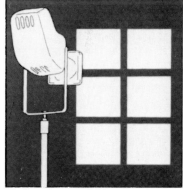

4 A gobo could be used to project a window shape or whatever is required

Luminaires

The Fresnel spot

The Fresnel spot takes its name from the Frenchman who originally designed the lens for use in lighthouses. At first it was mainly used by film studios and was rather expensive. Eventually, however, the price dropped and the Fresnel became more readily available. It is mechanically quite a simple instrument which produces a smooth wash of light.

The luminaire provides a soft-edged, ill-defined beam, which can be varied in size by moving the lamp and reflector towards or farther away from the lens.

The plano side of this lens has its surface cut away in steps to diffuse the light and is therefore called a stepped lens.

Unlike the profile spot, this luminaire has no gate. The luminaire is simply a box with a Fresnel lens at one end and a lamp and reflector which are both rigidly fixed to a plate. This plate can be made to slide along inside the box.

If beam shaping is required, a barn-door attachment can be fitted to the front of the luminaire. This usually consists of four independent doors or leaves, and can be rotated and angled to intercept and control the light.

These luminaires are ideal for lighting adjacent areas of the stage because the soft-edged beam means there will be no hard edges where the light beams merge. A small amount of flare exists outside the beam, but it is possible to lessen this effect by using a colouvred lens. This lens has blackened steps (or risers) which reduce any stray light and eliminate flare.

Flare occurs because the light passes through the steps at such a shallow angle it creates a spectral flare or rainbow, just like the effect of light passing through a prism.

Fresnel spots are normally available in 500 watt, 1000 watt, and 2000 watt sizes.

Focusing the Fresnel

Vary the beam width by movir the lamp and reflector nearer the lens for a bigger beam ang and farther away for a narrow beam angle.

Shape the beam of th luminaire with the barn doors

It is easier to find the center the beam if you first close th luminaire down to the smalle beam angle.

A Fresnel luminar

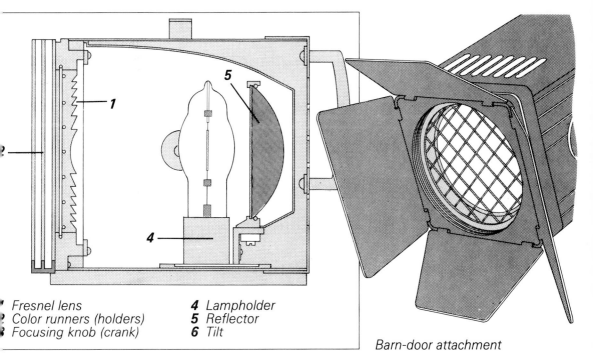

1 Fresnel lens
2 Color runners (holders)
3 Focusing knob (crank)
4 Lampholder
5 Reflector
6 Tilt

Barn-door attachment

e pebble-convex
minaire

pble-convex luminaires work
the same principal as the
snel luminaire, but this time
lens is a specially designed
no-convex lens. The back,
part of the lens is stippled
h bumps, which diffuses

the light passing through the
lens and makes the beam semi-
hard edged.

These luminaires have no flare
outside the beam. They are an
excellent substitute for profile
spotlights, if projection facilities
are not required. The barn doors
are used to shape the beam.

Focusing pebble-convex
spots

Vary the beam size by moving
the lamp and reflector nearer to
the lens for a larger beam angle,
and moving them farther away
for a smaller beam. Shape the
beam by using the barn doors.

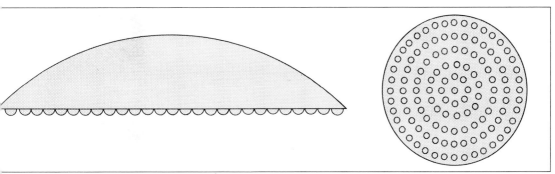

n and elevation of a pebble-convex lens

Luminaires

The Par

This luminaire provides an intense, virtually parallel, fixed beam of light and is rather like a car headlight. It consists of a lamp which has both a lens and reflector built into it. The luminaire shell is used to support the lamp and to keep flare to a minimum.

Pars are perfect for strong lighting effects such as bright sunlight through windows. Several used together on a batten (or border-light) can be useful as back or down light. A Par can also be an invaluable source of strong key light.

The lamps are 1000 watts, available in three beam widths; (9 x 12, 10 x 14, and 11 x 24 degrees) and 500 watts, which are available in four beam widths. Pars may also be available with 350 watt lamps.

Focusing Pars

It is necessary only to poin the Par in the right directio although because the beam oval-shaped, it may be rotate

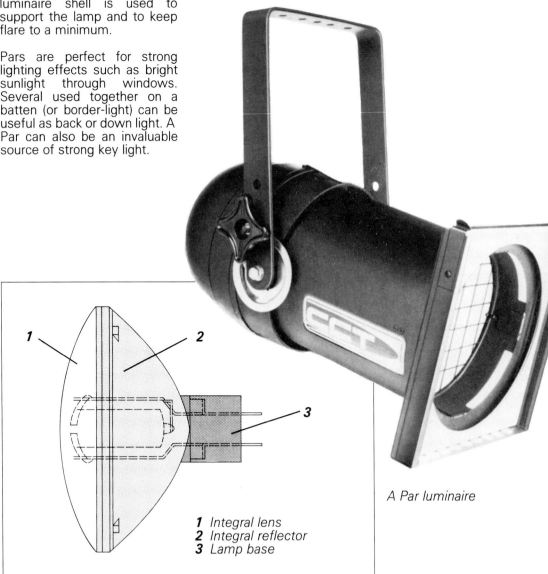

A Par luminaire

1 Integral lens
2 Integral reflector
3 Lamp base

Section of a Par lamp

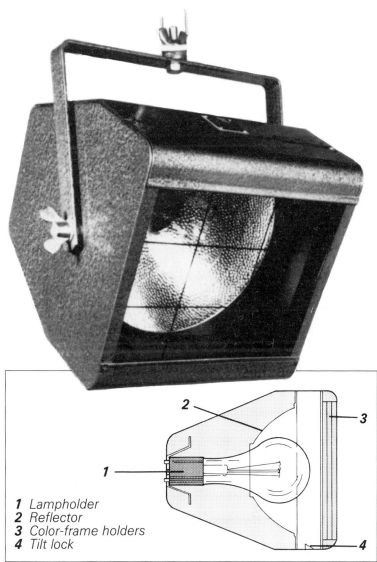

e Flood
flector floodlight

the name implies, floodlights
used to cover as large an
a as possible, to flood the
ge with light. They consist
ply of a lamp and reflector,
and are supplied with 150, 500,
and 1000 watt lamps. By using
veral of these units together,
becomes possible to light
ge backcloths or cycloramas.
cyclorama is a curved or
aight backcloth hung at the
r of the stage. It may be used
sky or background, painted
ite, and lit as required.

ere are three types of
odlighting. The first provides
even distribution of light (see
gram 1).

e second type of floodlight
vides more light at the
tom of the beam than in any
er part. This is achieved by
aping the reflector in a
mplex way and using an
taxial lamp, which is very
g with a filament that travels
ng its whole length (as
wn in diagram 2). These are
cellent for lighting backcloths
ere the luminaire is rigged
ar to the top of the cloth, and
en even illumination is
eded from top to bottom.

e third type of floodlighting is
a batten. Several lamps with
ectors are fixed together in
ctions to form a strip light.
en they are used on the
ge floor, they are called
und rows: when used on the
nt edge of the stage, they are
ed floats or footlights. When
tens are "flown" (suspended
ove the stage), they are
wn as magazine battens or
der lights.

1 Lampholder
2 Reflector
3 Color-frame holders
4 Tilt lock

Section of a floodlight

1 An evenly spread beam
of light

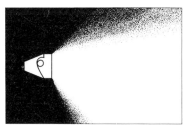

2 Light concentrated at the
bottom of the beam

33

Luminaires

Ground-row batten

Magazine batten (border light)

Luminaire maintenance

Luminaires are very delicate instruments and should be handled, and stored, with care. Unless they are maintained in good working order, the reflector and lamp may slip out of alignment and the instrument will not stay in position properly. Nothing is more irritating than trying to focus badly maintained luminaires.

Moreover, any old or worn electrical equipment can be potentially dangerous and so, whenever possible (perhaps in advance of a forthcoming production), carry out these three simple maintenance checks on each luminaire.

◇ To avoid an electric shock, always remember to unplug a luminaire before attempting to maintain it.

1 Electrical check:

Check cable tails visually for splits or breaks.

Check the plugs: the colored wires should go to the correct pins and all the terminal screws should be tight.

The cable's outer insulation should take the strain in the cable sheath grip (or clamp) so that the electrical connections inside the plug are not put under stress.

Color coding for Europe

The green/yellow wire is connected to the terminal marked **E (earth)**. The brown wire is connected to the terminal marked **L (live)**, and the blue wire is connected to the terminal marked **N (neutral)**.

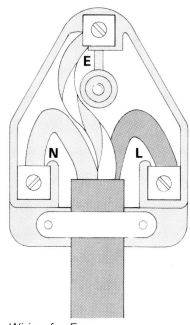

Wiring for Europe

Color coding for the USA

The black wire is connected the hot (live) terminal. T white or natural gray wire connected to the neut terminal, and the green wire connected to the safety grou (earth) terminal.

2 Optical check

Clean all the reflectors an lenses, and check that they a correctly positioned.

Make sure that the lamp properly positioned in th lampholder and trimmed in alignment.

3 Mechanical check

Ensure that' all the screw holding the luminaire togeth are tight.

Check that the tilt lock working correctly.

Check that the lens tube an focus knob (crank) move free

Check that the shutters mov freely but will remain whe positioned.

Make sure that the lantern has safety chain.

amps

ry luminaire needs a lamp to duce light. There are a ildering number of lamps lable, all with different tage sizes and lamp bases.

diagrams opposite show fundamental parts of a lamp the most common type of bases used in theater naires.

anging lamps

avoid an electric shock, ays unplug the luminaire ore changing a lamp.

nove a blown lamp with t care as occasionally the s envelope can shatter. sp the lamp by the base, or it carefully with a soft cloth glove.

ays ensure the correct acement lamp is used, as cified for the luminaire.

ot forget to wear the plastic e or shroud supplied with new lamp. Never touch the s envelope as any greasy sture from your hands will act heat and this could melt glass, resulting in an osion. If lamps have been ched, it is advisable to clean n with neat alcohol or hylated spirit.

not forget to remove the ud when the lamp is ectly positioned in its pholder.

np bases

re are three types of lamp e most commonly used in ter luminaires but each is available in two or three rent sizes.

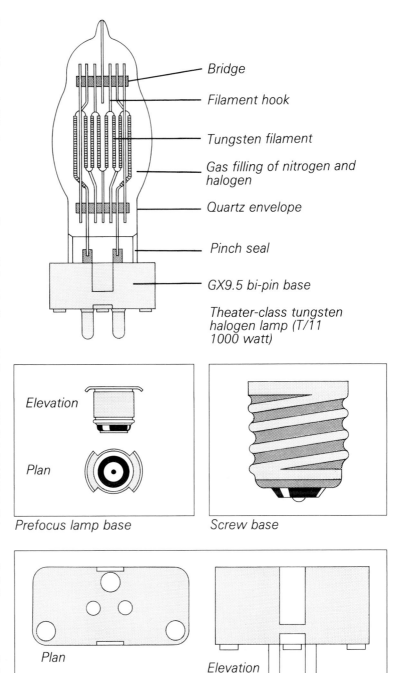

Bridge

Filament hook

Tungsten filament

Gas filling of nitrogen and halogen

Quartz envelope

Pinch seal

GX9.5 bi-pin base

Theater-class tungsten halogen lamp (T/11 1000 watt)

Elevation

Plan

Prefocus lamp base

Screw base

Plan

Elevation

Bi-pin lamp base

Dimmers

Control of the lighting during a performance is a fundamental requirement, and dimmers are the nerve center of any lighting control system. If the play requires a gradual transition from a black-out to full brightness (or vice-versa), dimmers provide the means to fade luminaires up and down.

The dimmers of today often use an electronic device called an SCR (silicon controlled rectifier). This device belongs to the thyristor family of semiconductor devices, which are simply switching devices. In order to fully understand the way dimmers work, some basic electrical knowledge is necessary (see pages 150-157).

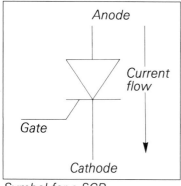

Symbol for a SCR

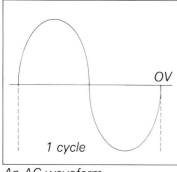

An AC waveform

The electricity supply consists of an alternating current. This means that the supply alternates above positive(+) and below negative(-) zero volts, making a complete cycle fifty or sixty times every second.

Two SCRs are required to control AC (alternating current), as current can pass only one way through them. Therefore, the pair of SCRs are wired "back to back", one controlling the positive (+) half of the cycle, and the other controlling the negative (-) half. With the fader at full (level 10), the AC waveform remains pure. This is because the SCRs are allowing full current to pass through by switching on at the start of each half-cycle. But, as the fader is brought down, then the point at which the SCRs turn on moves farther up the half cycle. This is called "phase control".

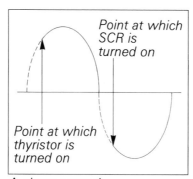

A phase control

SCRs can be turned off only by preventing the current passing through. This will happen automatically with an AC waveform, with each half-cycle starting at 0 volts, peaking to maximum, and then dropping back to 0 volts. Triacs are used in some dimmers and are similar to two SCRs.

Only one is needed to con an AC waveform. By usin trigger control to switch on SCRs via the gate at the corr time, it is possible to regul the current progressively, required. The trigger con circuit is controlled by a "fad on a lighting board.

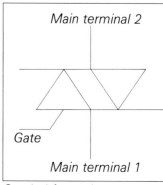

Symbol for a triac

Setting up dimmers

There are normally only t adjustments that can be ma These utilize either:

1 The relationship between mains voltage at dimmer out and the control voltage from lighting desk: fader at level

2 The relationship between reduced mains voltage dimmer output and the con voltage from the lighting de fader at level 0.

These adjustments should o be made in strict accordar with the instructions from manufacturer.

Note: Care must be taken w these two adjustments as dimmers will be switched while these checks are be carried out.

Manual preset lighting boards

anual lighting boards provide fader for each dimmer or hannel, thereby allowing each mmer to have its own dependent control. To help e operator to fade a lighting ate up or down, another fader, lled a master, is used to ontrol the level of output from ich channel fader to its own mmer. This collection of annel faders and a master is lled a preset.

is possible to set a lighting ate on the preset without the hting being seen on stage vith the master at level 0). hen, when a lighting cue is ecuted, the master is raised to level 10 (or full) and the lighting state is achieved on stage. At this point, if any more lighting states are required, channel faders will have to be moved during the performance by hand to modify the existing lighting. Add more presets, and several lighting states can be preset ahead and then played back by fading from one preset to another, using submasters.

Most manual boards have more than one master per preset. To avoid confusion, these can be labeled A or B, red or white, and so on. Above each channel fader is located a multi-position switch, which enables it to be switched to any submaster . This allows more than one lighting state to be set up on one preset, and is known as grouping. The manual board shown is a three-preset, three-group lighting desk or consul.

Using manual systems

As the channel levels have to be written down, it can be very useful to use a "dedicated" cue sheet (one which is designed for a specific lighting board), presenting a clear view of levels and grouping. On page 38 is a cue sheet designed for a thirty-six way, three-preset, two-group manual board.

Rank Strand three-preset, three-group, manual–lighting control system

Manual cue sheet

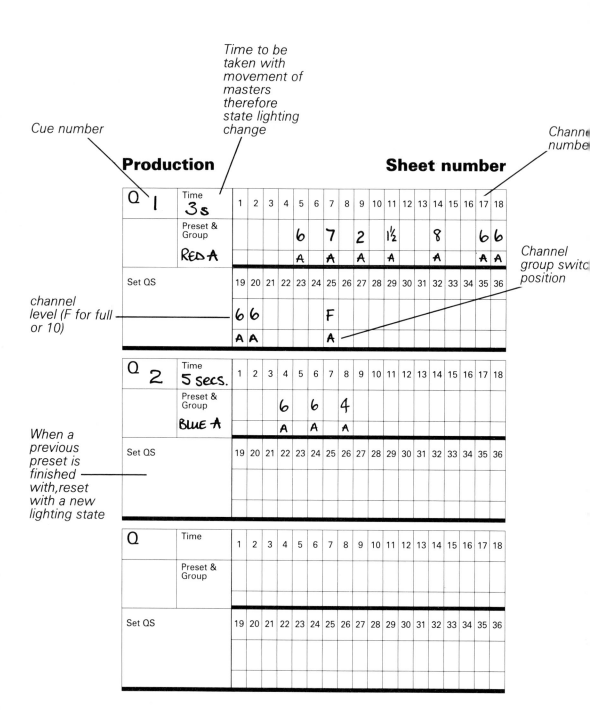

Typical cue sheet for a thirty-six way, three-preset, two-group manual board

Time		1	2	3	4	5	6	7	8	9	10	11	12	13	14	15	16	17	18
Preset & Group																			
Set QS		19	20	21	22	23	24	25	26	27	28	29	30	31	32	33	34	35	36

Time		1	2	3	4	5	6	7	8	9	10	11	12	13	14	15	16	17	18
Preset & Group																			
Set QS		19	20	21	22	23	24	25	26	27	28	29	30	31	32	33	34	35	36

Time		1	2	3	4	5	6	7	8	9	10	11	12	13	14	15	16	17	18
Preset & Group																			
Set QS		19	20	21	22	23	24	25	26	27	28	29	30	31	32	33	34	35	36

39

Computer memory lighting control

Computer memory boards have revolutionized stage lighting techniques. The tedium of writing down detailed lighting plots is now removed and the whole process of lighting is quicker and more flexible.

Memory boards provide the facility to instantly play back a lighting state and reproduce it exactly, level for level. Also they can be used to fade or switch rapidly through many different lighting states, just as fast as you can push the buttons.

Moreover, a memory board saves a great deal of time during lighting sessions and rehearsals. Instead of writing down individual levels, one push of a record button will memorize the current lighting state and there is no need to wait for the board operator to set up possibly twenty or thirty faders. Entering a memory number and pushing a cross-fade button is all that is required to play back a lighting state.

Today memory boards are true computers, using computer memory RAM (random access memory) and floppy disks for storing lighting states, as well as cassettes or even cartridges.

As computers are purely digital devices, the output to dimmers is stepped. The more expensive boards can have over two hundred and fifty different steps between levels 0 and 10; the cheaper variety as few as thirty-two.

On slow fades, if the steps are too few, the audience may be aware of the switching of the dimmers through each step. This is obviously undesirable because the lighting will look jerky, so the more steps, the better the result.

The first memory system shown here is Rank Strand's "M24", which is eminently suitable for use in a small

theater, a school, or an amate dramatic society.

It can control sixty dimmers a is able to memorize nea two hundred different lightin states. Six different cues c be controlled simultaneously different recorded speeds, a a sequence of over fifty time cues can be automatically run succession.

As well as memorizing all th lighting in this way, the control systems allow operator to take immedia action if need be. The lighting stage can be instantaneous altered if an operator electrician chooses, so in r way need operators fear th the whole process has bee taken out of their hands.

Obviously such systems are f more advanced than a manual board, and all th buttons and controls mig

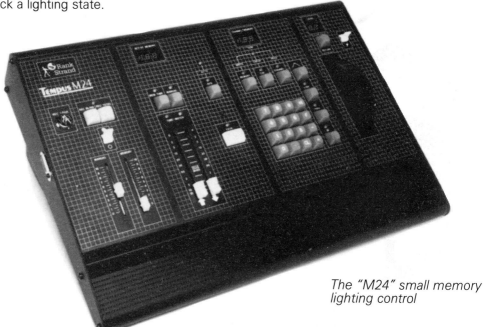

The "M24" small memory lighting control

em rather confusing and mplicated at first. They are, wever, relatively simple to erate and the electrician will bably discover how to use basic controls surprisingly ckly. As the whole thing comes more familiar, he or e will be able to experiment h the more advanced nements such machines e to offer.

fact, once the electrician or rd operator is able to fully ploit the new system, the ole process of a lighting earsal will be very much cker. In fact, the lighting signer may have to adapt vailing methods drastically in ler to keep up!

Memory systems like these are quite small and so have the added advantage of being readily transported if the show goes "on tour".

As new developments and advances in the technology of lighting memory systems are taking place all the time, up-to-date information must be obtained from manufacturers before deciding which system will suit your needs and budget.

The other memory control system shown here is Rank Strand's top of the line "Galaxy" system, a rather more complex and expensive piece of equipment. However, a very wide range of systems is now

being produced and small theater companies need not automatically assume that these systems will be beyond their budget!

Computerized lighting control systems represent the very sophisticated equipment which is available today. However, in order to create your own stage lighting, you will need to be familiar with the requirements of the particular stage you are planning to light, and with whatever equipment is already available there or within the budget to buy. Only then can you plan for future productions, and decide which control system is most suitable for your specific needs.

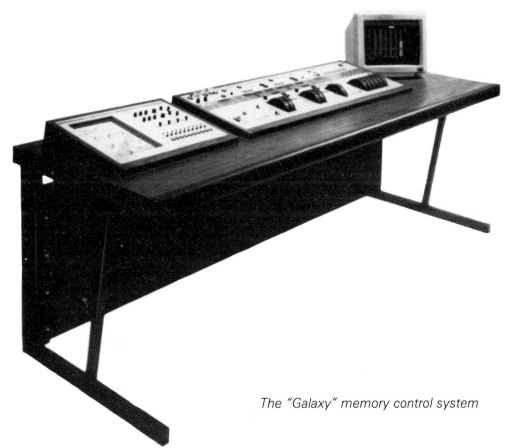

The "Galaxy" memory control system

Patching

In lighting circles, the term patching refers to a different system of "plugging up" the lighting, whereby a luminaire is plugged into a socket, which in turn is wired direct to a dimmer.

With patching, a luminaire is plugged into a socket. The socket is wired to a plug that fits into a patch panel. When required, this plug can be moved to a socket in the patch panel which is wired to a dimmer. This system is most commonly used in the USA, although similar systems do exist in England and Europe.

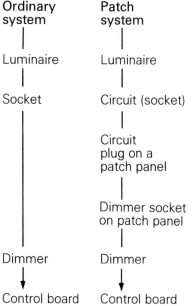

Ordinary system	Patch system
|	|
Luminaire	Luminaire
|	|
Socket	Circuit (socket)
|	|
	Circuit plug on a patch panel
	|
	Dimmer socket on patch panel
	|
Dimmer	Dimmer
↓	↓
Control board	Control board

At first this may seem an unnecessarily involved way of doing things. However, a well-designed patch system can save a great deal of time when cabling up luminaires. It can also make the whole process of "plugging-up" more versatile.

Take, for example, a small theater which has been wired up in the conventional manner with twenty-four dimmers and twenty-four luminaires. Each of the luminaires can be plugged into one of the twenty-four socket outlets around the theater. Each socket is then wired to one of the dimmers so that one socket is allocated to one dimmer. Imagine that twelve of these circuits or sockets are for the stage, and twelve for the front-of-house luminaires in the auditorium.

This, on the surface, appears to be a good workable system. The first twelve luminaires can be used on stage, and the other twelve for front-of-house.

However, should a situation arise when the set is built rather far to the front so that the lighting has to be set down-stage, then difficulties arise. All the luminaires may have to be rigged front-of-house and all may require separate circuits. This complication can be resolved only if twelve of the luminaires are cabled back to the socket outlets on the stage.

Although feasible, such an undertaking can be awkward, time-consuming, and also quite expensive as long cable runs will be needed.

Now imagine the same theater with the same number of dimmers and luminaires, but this time with a patch system. If the system incorporated forty-eight socket outlets in the theater, which were wired back to a patch panel, then there could be twenty-four sockets front-of-house and twenty-four on stage.

Any one of these forty-ei outlets could then be patche plugged into one of the twel four sockets on the patch pa These sockets, in turn, wired to the dimmers.

Thus all twenty-four lumina could be used with no probl being either plugged on stag at front-of-house. By patch on the patch panel, each car allocated its own dimmer. is just one example of the the apparently complica patching system can simp matters. The complications already "built-in" so to spea

Patching is also useful pairing. If two luminaires required to share the sa dimmer, but are on oppo: sides of the auditorium, this present a problem.

If, however, a patch systen being used, then the probl does not exist in the same w The luminaires can be plugg to the nearest circuit and tl they can be paired (or "gange at the patch panel. This can done by plugging the t corresponding patch plugs i one patch socket, using splitter (or adapter). Some pa panels will have a multi-soc arrangement for each dimr in order to accommo several patch plugs.

In some theaters the pa systems are so large that th may be literally hundreds circuits. It is essential to ke track of exactly what equipm has been plugged and just h and where this has been do Make a chart or keep a recor hook-up schedule) of this, that if any faults occur these be dealt with quickly.

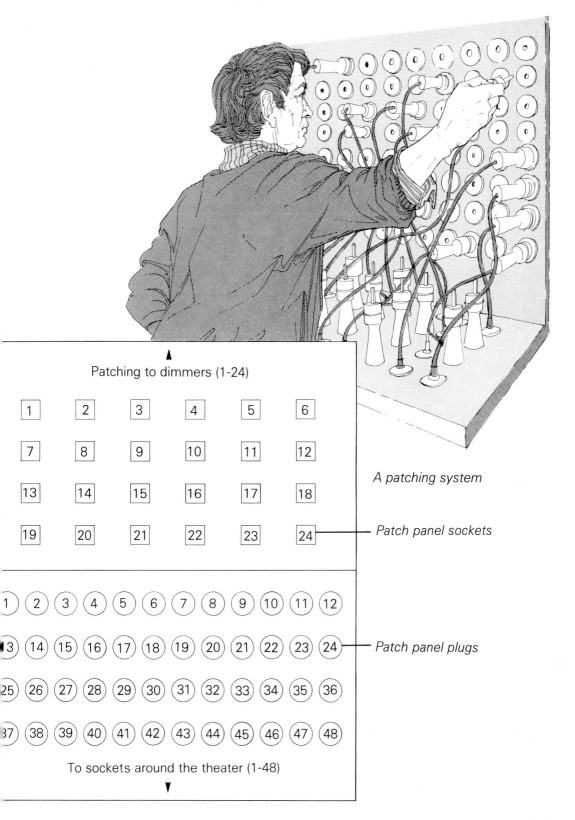

Patching to dimmers (1-24)

1	2	3	4	5	6
7	8	9	10	11	12
13	14	15	16	17	18
19	20	21	22	23	24

A patching system

Patch panel sockets

1 2 3 4 5 6 7 8 9 10 11 12
13 14 15 16 17 18 19 20 21 22 23 24
25 26 27 28 29 30 31 32 33 34 35 36
37 38 39 40 41 42 43 44 45 46 47 48

Patch panel plugs

To sockets around the theater (1-48)

Basic techniques

All the different luminaires discussed in the previous section are the tools of the lighting designer. Before they can be properly used to light the actor and the stage and to create a visual concept, the designer must understand the basic techniques of lighting.

Lighting structures

The way the light from each luminaire is made to fall upon the stage or an actor alters its structure fundamentally. Side light, top light, back light, and so on we shall refer to as lighting "structures". The manner in which these structures can change the appearance of people or objects on the stage means that light really can be used as a modeling medium.

Flat front light

If flat front light is used in isolation and shines directly into the actor's face, it flattens the features and looks very bland.

However, it is useful when an unavoidably high key light has made an actor's eyes disappear into the shadows cast by the upper part of the eye socket. This is when front lighting at a flat angle can alleviate the problem and is often used as an "eye-socket filler"! Never set the intensity level too high, or ugly shadows will be cast on the up-stage part of the set.

Front light at 45 degrees

Place the front lights at a 45 degree angle and they instantly become more flattering. This is the beginning of "portrait" lighting and also creates good cover for the acting area.

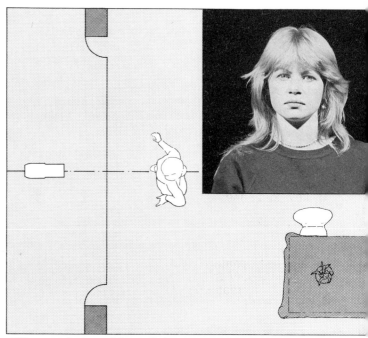

Effect and plan of front light

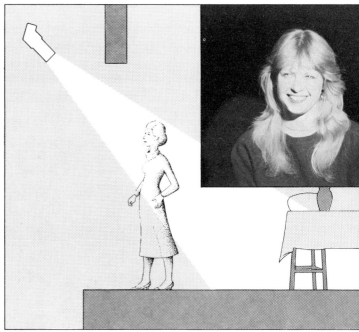

Effect and elevation of 45° front light

a rule, the object of the exercise is to light the actor, particularly his or her face. To do this most naturally, a spotlight should be rigged approximately 45 degrees above and 45 degrees to the side of the actor's face. By using two spotlights, one on each side at this 45 degree angle, harsh shadows will be avoided.

Key and fill light

The terms "key light" and "fill light" describe the direction and intensity of the lights being used. A key light provides the main source of light in any scene and the fill light, appropriately, fills the areas of shadow that this main key light also creates. (See also pages 83-84.)

Side light

Side lighting may be considered the second most important structure to use when lighting an actor. Side light is created, more or less, as soon as the luminaire moves to one side of the vertical plane, above the actor or object being lit.

If the angle of side light used is very shallow or horizontal to the actor, then it may be termed "cross light". It will usually emanate from the wings of the stage, with the luminaires rigged on booms, ladders, or stands. If required, it can be made to cross the stage from one side to the other, without lighting the stage floor.

In general, side light helps to mould and sculpture the actor on stage. It lights the actor's face when he or she faces the wings. Without side lighting, or backlighting, the actor's face

would otherwise be plunged into shadow when turned away from the audience. Side light also makes a very useful key light. For instance, in a box set, a strong side light could be used at the side of the stage where a window is supposed to be, as though sun or moonlight is streaming in.

Side lighting at head height is sometimes used for special dramatic effects as it edges or "rims" the actor's body with light. This is particularly useful for dance or ballet. It does, however, look unnatural, and has the disadvantage that the performers may cast shadows upon each other.

Elevation of 45° side light

Effect of horizontal side light

Effect of 45° side light

Basic techniques

Back light

Back light has several functions. First it will add to the sculpturing qualities of a design. If there is a high proportion of back light above and behind the actor, the beams will create a halo on the head and shoulders. This helps to separate the actors from the background.

It should also be noted that back light will not affect an actor's face. This can be very useful when the stage needs to be heavily colored with a light which would normally alter the skin tones of an actor. By using the strong color as back light, and normal skin-tone colors for the front light, dramatic stage color changes can be made without turning the actor bright green or red! He will of course, have a colored "halo" on the head and shoulders, but this is acceptable.

The whole mood of a scene can be altered by the use of differently colored backlight washes, indeed, it is by the use of backlight that atmosphere can be created. Light is added from the front to light the stage so the actor can be seen.

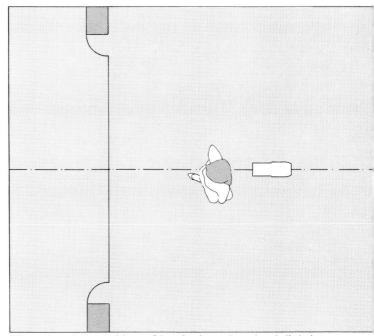

Plan showing position of luminaire when back lighting

Back light shown in elevation

Effect of back light

p or down light

or down light should not be
nfused with back light.
hough similar in its overall
aracteristics, top light will
ke protruding body and facial
tures. It has excellent
lpturing qualities and is
ful for high contrast work.

cause of its literally striking
ility, the effect of top light
be quite dramatic. Lighting
fully-armored soldier from
ectly above will expose only
tain elements of the
stume: perhaps a protruding
ger or sword, or his
astplate and headgear.

decision to use either top
t or back light is therefore
pendent on the design quality
uired.

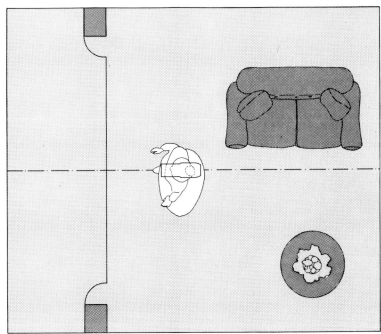

Plan showing position of luminaire when top or down lighting

ect of top light

Top light shown in elevation

Basic techniques

Bottom or up light

Bottom or up light looks very unnatural and is rarely used today, unless it is the only way a particular special or dramatic effect can be achieved — such as actors grouped around a candle on the floor or sitting beside a camp fire.

Many years ago, bottom light was quite commonplace with the use of "floats" — so-called because the light here was once provided by oilwicks floating in water to lessen the risk of fire! Footlights (lights running across the front of the stage at floor level) can be categorized as bottom light.

Float positions can still be found in a lot of theaters today. These often consist simply of holes or slots in the forestage, normally covered with stage flooring. This flooring can be removed when the float position is required. The lighting designer is then able to insert lights to focus upwards, thereby lighting actors or scenery from below.

The effect of a single light uplighting an actor's face can be eerie and quite spectacular.

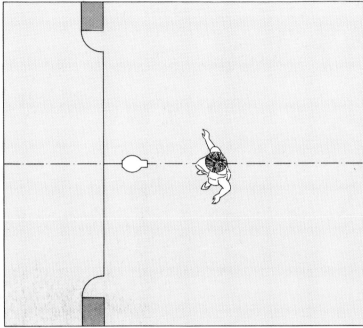

Plan showing position of luminaire when uplighting

Effect of up light

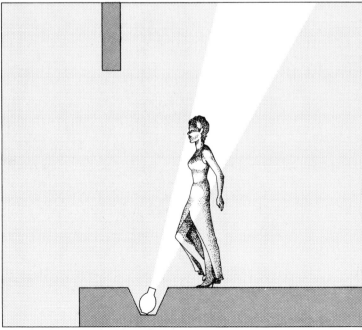

Up light shown in elevation

e use of a float batten (when
veral lights are fixed together)
I give a more general and
ntle up light. This is still used
some "old-fashioned" style
oductions — perhaps a
torian melodrama, or a
storation piece. The quality
this light will usually add
thenticity to sets and
stumes. Also, the color of the
or stage can be subtly
ered by the use of subdued
otlighting.

ntomime is another type of
oduction that may benefit
m the use of floats. Scenic
ths can often take on a
ferent character when lit
m below rather than above.

ttom light is also used to
eat effect to create an
rizon, or perhaps a sunrise or
nset behind a scenic ground
v. Because the most intense
ht is near the base of the
clorama, a great illusion of
tance can be created by
hting between a scenic
ound row and a sky-cloth or
clorama. A set designer will
rmally leave sufficient space
tween the two pieces of set
allow for this.

ound-row sections usually
me wired either in a two or
ee-circuit combination. It is
ssible, with several sections
ground row, to have a three-
or wash from below on to the
clorama (such as daylight,
nrise, and sunset).

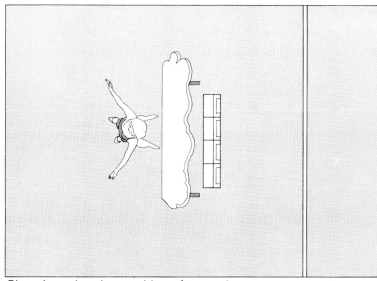

Plan view showing position of ground row

Ground row lighting shown in elevation

unset	Daylight	Sunrise	Sunset	Daylight	Sunrise	Sunset	Daylight	Sunrise

hree-color-wash ground row

Basic techniques

Silhouette

A silhouette, when required, is achieved by lighting just the background and nothing else. Obviously, unlit people or objects positioned in front of the background will then appear as dark outlines and shapes or silhouettes.

If the silhouette is to appear in front of a cloth or cyclorama, it is best to backlight the material, if possible, providing that the material is of the correct type. Back lighting prevents ambient light from bouncing around and will create a sharper silhouette.

It is not always necessary to light a solid background to create a silhouette. Back lighting a smoke screen behind an actor will create a stunning silhouette, with the image being "shadow projected" in the smoke. This use of shadow imaging is used a great deal in laser-light design.

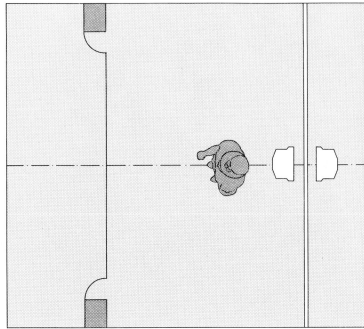

Plan showing position of luminaire for silhouette lighting

Effect created by silhouette lighting

Silhouette light shown in elevation

...unning silhouette produced by using a back-lit smoke screen

Small beginnings

The lighting techniques which are discussed throughout this book will apply to all theaters, large and small, professional and amateur. However, the equipment that might be used to light the stage will vary enormously, and a very new or young organization with a small budget may consider that a great deal which has been discussed so far is beyond their capabilities or budget.

The chapter on *Lighting the stage with limited resources* explores many techniques that may be used to overcome some of these problems, and so make the most of what is available.

None the less, the beginner may well feel that some of the basic questions still remain unanswered. It is all too easy to assume that everything has been fully explained, to take for granted that everybody is fully conversant with the fundamentals and familiar with the normal lighting jargon. In this way the more basic but essential information may be overlooked.

Knowing just how to begin, finding out what is strictly essential for a first production, choosing, hiring, or buying new lighting, and then achieving a good result with perhaps as few as half a dozen luminaires; this is precisely the sort of information that is often sadly lacking but which the beginner needs to know.

Moreover the professional, to might discover there is much learn; a village hall or sch production would probably as daunting a possibility someone used to sophisticat equipment as it is for the lighti "expert" who has just be coerced into lighting a play the very first time!

Note: It will be useful to draw a cue sheet for each producti There is an example of a man cue sheet on page 39. In ord that this may be photocopie copyright regulations applyi to the rest of the book ha been released for that page.

How to begin?

What luminaires should the beginner choose?

It is not theater size alone which determines the choice of luminaire. Finances, lighting positions, power supply, and individual preference may well be the first considerations.

The Fresnel has an extremely versatile beam angle and is able to give a small "pool" or "spot" of light, or it can easily be "flooded" so as to cover a much wider area of the stage.

Profiles are also very useful when front-of-house positions are some distance from the stage. They are easier to control and will project gobos, which Fresnels are unable to do. Even so, their overall flexibility of beam angles will not compete with the Fresnel.

Some floodlights would al be very useful for cyclorar lighting and for lighting t stage behind the proscenium arch. They light a wide area stage at a short distance, rath than providing a narrow beam light, (although it should remembered that the light fr a flood is very uncontrollable

Should footlights be used they are already available

Footlights should not be us simply because they are ther Certainly they can be used if t show particularly calls for the perhaps for a Victorian mus hall, a Restoration piece, or lighting the curtain (the tab:

Can luminaires be hired?

Luminaires may be rented bu is important to know exac what is required. Contact t rental company in advance inform them of your speci requirements and also tell the which alternatives would acceptable (in case they cann provide every item requested Remember that insurance very important. Most ren companies hold the custom personally responsible, so try insure against every possib mishap, including accident damage, theft, and fire.

What does up stage, sta right, and so on mean?

These expressions describe t geography of a stage. If an act is positioned stage right, then seen from the auditorium, he she will be on the left-hand si of the stage. The plan he shows all the different areas the stage and the terms that a used to describe them.

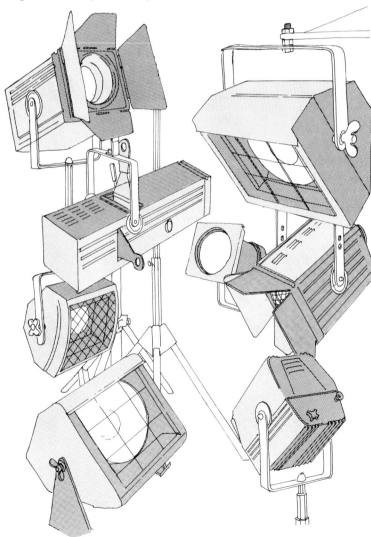

Cyclorama

EMIGRATING NEW YORK

Up stage right

Up stage center

Up stage left

Wings

Wings

Center right

Center stage

Center left

Wings

Wings

Down stage right

Down stage center

Down stage left

reas of the stage

Avoiding accidents

How do you use safety chains and what are the legal requirements?

Safety chains should be fitted as a matter of course to all the luminaires. If the instrument is very heavy, make sure the chain is taut. A luminaire which is restrained by a slack chain would be badly jolted if it fell and this could cause breakage or might dislodge any fittings such as an iris or gobo. Legal requirements vary from city to city. Some authorities insist on safety chains being fixed to all luminaires hung above an audience. The Greater London Council rules that chains should be fitted to all luminaires. Always check local regulations, but in any event, use safety chains whenever possible.

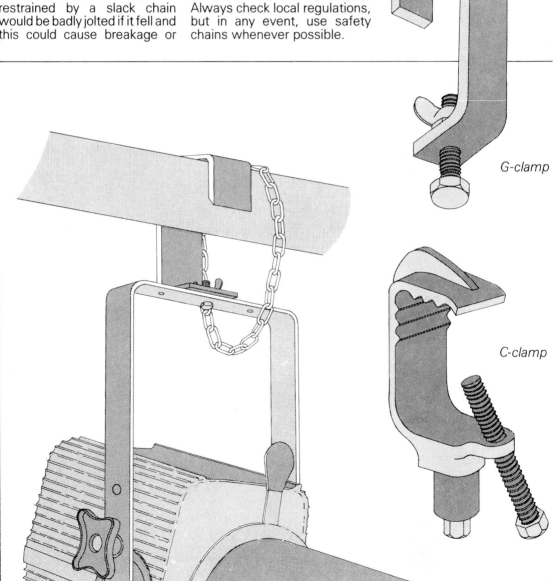

G-clamp

C-clamp

■at ladders are best to ■e when rigging?

■e a new inverted Y-shaped ■der or a conventional A-■aped one. These are the most ■ble, but make sure they can ■ch the required height. Using ■ extending ladder will be ■her dangerous if it is erected ■ainst movable scenery.

■w do fire regulations ■ect lighting? Are lights ■ stands safe?

■ain, fire regulations differ ■m city to city. Generally, ■les should be kept clear. If ■y are being used near the ■blic, then the luminaires ■uld be securely fixed or ■ighted down. This is ■mething that should be ■cussed in the early planning ■ges with the production or ■ge manager and the fire ■thorities. Do not wait until the ■up, when it may be too late to ■d another alternative.

■n insulation tape be ■ed?

■ulation tape should never be ■ed to splice power cables ■gether. Always use proper ■nnecting devices (preferably ■lug and socket).

■ "bean-can" luminaires ■e?

■ean or biscuit-tin luminaire is ■htly vulnerable because it ■s such a thin frame or case. ■id using these home-made ■ps if they are likely to be ■ked or could be knocked by ■avy scenery. Normally they ■uld not need a guard over the ■nt. This is covered in greater ■ail on page 149.

◇ Are naked lamps a fire risk?

Naked lamps should not touch any scenery or drapes. Even though these items should be fire-proofed, a naked lamp, and even the luminaire itself, can become very hot and may singe even a fire-resistant material.

A Light collapsible stand with four telescopic tubes, each with wing nuts for securing

B Heavy-based telescopic stand with one extension

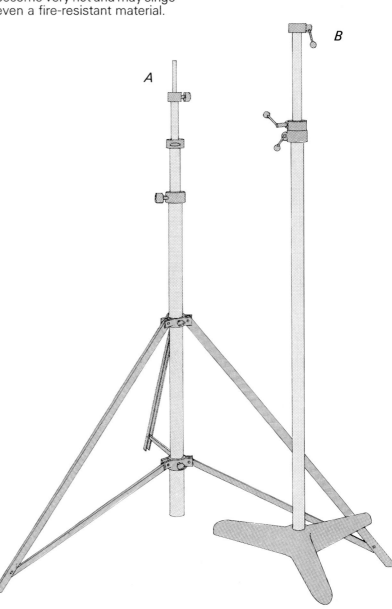

57

Using the luminaires

What is a follow spot and how is it used?

A follow spot is usually a profile spotlight which is operated manually to follow the actors, singers, or dancers on stage. It sits on a specially designed stand which enables it to achieve a smooth sideways movement. The spotlight will often have an iris to make the beam larger or smaller. It may also have a color magazine (to facilitate quick color changes) as well as some form of dimmer and black-out mechanism.

Most luminaires which are designed as follow spots have all these capabilities as part of their basic design. However, some of the arc-lamp follow spots (such as an HMI or Xenon carbon arc) cannot be dimmed from the light source but may be fitted instead with a mechanical dimming system which will provide this facility if required.

When using a follow spot with a light source other than tungsten it will be advisable to color-correct the light emitted back to that of tungsten. There are several filters which can do this, such as Lee 237 and Lee 238.

Follow-spots are expensive, so it is worth noting that any narrow-angle profile can be used as a substitute. It may be advisable to bolt a handle to the case of the luminaire as this can become very hot. The "follow spot" will then be much easier to manipulate. To control the size of the beam, put an iris into the "gate" and slide a piece of black card in front of the luminaire. This will then enable dimming or black-out to be successfully achieved.

How can you obtain the best results from just six or eight luminaires?

Providing that the basic rule of lighting is followed, (that is lighting at 45 degrees from the horizontal and vertical plane), then shadows should not occur. These are normally caused by using too low a lighting angle. Divide the stage up into a grid (rows and columns). Each section should be about one "light-pool" from corner corner diagonally. (One "light pool" is the diameter of the light spread from only one luminaire.

In order to light the area in front of the proscenium arch and the downstage sections, four of the luminaires should be positioned in pairs at the ends of the front-of-house bar (pipe). Two further luminaires rigged on a bar behind the proscenium arch will light the upstage sections.

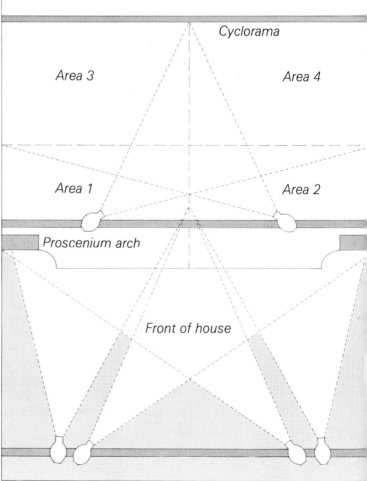

Shadows can be avoided, even with only six luminaires

Where should battens be?

The best place for a batten (strip light) is about one meter away from the cloth or border it is to light. If the batten is too close, then the shadows made by wrinkles or folds in the cloth may appear. If the batten is too far away, the intensity of light is lost and there will be light spill on the surrounding areas.

How many spot bars (pipes) are necessary?

There should be sufficient bar (pipe) space to support the luminaires needed for front lighting. Back and side lighting can be used for the remaining effects if space is at a premium.

How are luminaires masked?

The masking or concealing of luminaires is usually the set designer's task, but early meetings with the rest of the production team will help to achieve mutually desirable masking arrangements. Spot bars are often masked with borders and the designer will decide where to place these by working out the "sightlines", so that the bars are hidden, even to those sitting in the front row.

What is gauze and how is gauze used?

Gauze is a large-weave cloth which is useful for special effects (see page 121).

How is spill light avoided?

Light spill into the auditorium is usually caused by badly focused back light. A simple way to avoid this is to check the effect by sitting in the front row when the back light is focused. Then you can ensure the audience will not be blinded, and the shutters or barn doors can be adjusted to restrict the light to the stage edge. Ambient spill also occurs if front-of-house Fresnels are used from a position too far from the stage.

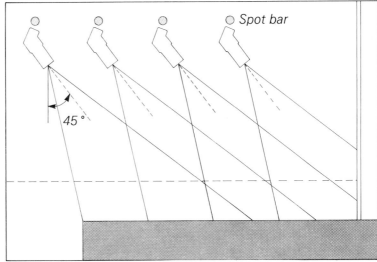
Four spot bars providing frontlight cover

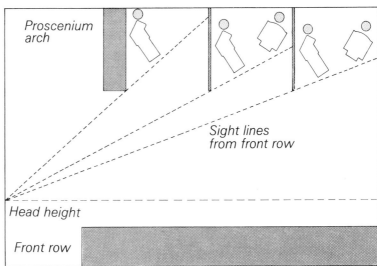
Lighting rig masked with borders which conceal the luminaires

How is the auditorium lit?

House lights are normally part of the fabric of the building, but it is preferable to have two sets of lights: bright lights for normal use when there is no show (working lights), plus a set of lights that can be faded.

59

Color and special effects

What filters should be purchased?

Basic color will be needed for day, night, and so on. The choice will be dependant on the color of set, cyclorama, or backcloth that is being lit. Below is the list of Lee color numbers that may generally be used and should suit most circumstances:

Warm
Daylight: 103,159,212,206,205, open white

Cool
Daylight: 117,201,202,203,218

Moonlight: 143,161,174,183

Indoor:
103,151,152,153,154,162, open white

Street: as above (day/night)

Countryside/woodland: composite of ambers/golds

How are gobos used? Is it possible to make them?

Gobos can be used to project patterns and images, including tower-block lights, stars, or in fact anything you wish, on to a backcloth or curtain. Beware, however, as gobos can only be used in profile spotlights and have to be inserted between the lamp and the focusing lens, which is called the "gate". It is possible to make your own gobo. This is fully described in the *Special Effects* section.

Is projection possible?

Yes, projection can be used successfully in an amateur production. Normally a simple domestic projector will suffice but obviously, if used in a bright lighting state, it may not be bright enough. The use of slide projection has been covered in greater detail in the *Special Effects* section.

Can fluorescent paint be used? Are ultra-violet lamps legal?

Fluorescent paint will w effectively if used under ul violet light alone. Its use is qu legal, but if it is not available, t primary blue filter to a lumina to provide a poor substitute.

Can lighting be a "substitute" for costume or set?

This has been done in r concerts and for some da productions. Lighting may h to suggest time and loca especially when the set is v basic. Perhaps, one day, las and holograms will be used project sets.

How can lighting effect a scene change?

When stage hands are sce changing, using break-up got would create a more interest lighting state.

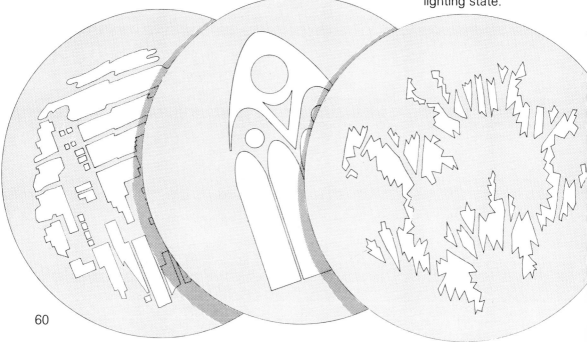

Problems and afterthoughts

How is a practical rigged?

A "practical", such as a table or standard lamp, should, when possible, be plugged into a circuit that is connected to the control board and not switched on or off by the actors on stage. In this way the required light changes can be co-ordinated.

How may a member of the audience be lit?

For lighting a member of the audience, a spotlight can be used. This must be pre-focused and is called a special (see page). To light someone entering the auditorium, a follow spot would be rather better.

What should the control-board operator do if an actor jumps six pages?

It is not the lighting designer's problem if several pages are suddenly omitted. The stage manager, or a prompt who has the book to hand, will advise and instruct all the relevant departments, such as lighting and sound, hopefully in a co-ordinated manner.

If a memory board is in use then this is no problem. The necessary memory, with its appropriate lighting state, can be readily called up and activated when the stage manager or prompt so instructs.

If a manual board is in use, then the operator will have to advise that he or she will require thirty seconds (or whatever time is necessary to set the relevant state) and then inform them when it is set. Co-ordination with the person "on the book" and making sure clear and appropriate cues are given will be vital at such moments if chaos is to be avoided.

How do you light the house tab (curtain)?

This is one situation where footlights would be ideal. If no footlights are available, then front lights positioned either side of the proscenium arch will suffice. At the beginning of the performance, any lighting of the house tab should be faded out slightly later than the auditorium lights, thus drawing audience attention to the stage.

How can a mirror be used without causing reflection problems?

Sometimes a small adjustment to the angle of the mirror will solve the problem. There is also a selection of low-reflective sprays on the market which will prevent glare. Alternatively the mirror can be lightly smeared with petroleum jelly or soap.

What are the most common lighting mistakes a beginner makes?

Often the beginner lights the set rather than lighting the actor. Reading the section on *Lighting the stage* (on pages 62-89) with its explanation of how to organize the lighting of the acting area, should be of considerable help.

Another common error is to frontlight with too much dense color. Tints should always be used for frontlighting.

Frontlighting a woodland scene in green — WRONG

Frontlighting a sunny day in strong yellow — WRONG

Frontlighting a night scene in very deep blue — WRONG

Therefore be careful with color and follow the guidelines in *Color* (pages 100-111).

Can one person successfully design and light a production?

John Bury designs and lights productions most successfully. A scenographer is the name usually applied to someone who is responsible for all aspects of stage design. In the United States, in fact, the areas of training often overlap.

Should smoking be permitted?

Smoking will not usually affect lighting but nowadays most theaters ban smoking for social reasons and because of the high fire risk.

What special or extra item should a company buy if left an unexpected legacy?

So much depends on the size and type of the company — it is difficult to generalize on this. It would be best to consult with the various manufacturers and exploit their knowledge to ascertain the requirements of a particular theater.

As these questions and answers show, there are not necessarily any "hard and fast" rules to follows. Often it is a case of preference or conditions imposed by the venue, but a great deal of fun can be gained in finding the solution.

Lighting the stage

Pre-planning

To light any production in a pleasing way and to achieve all the effects that the lighting designer, the set and costume designers, and the director require, and at the same time to be well organized, takes considerable time and thought.

Ideally, the lighting plan should evolve and grow from the early pre-planning stage, in order to contribute most effectively to the production.

Strangely, it comes as a surprise to some people that every luminaire used in a lighting rig will have been pre-planned before the production is really under way. It is not simply a case of rigging up any instrument into any available space and hoping you will have enough of both. Each luminaire will have its own place and its own specific job to do.

When in a professional situation methodical pre-planning is vital, and the lighting designer will have a much easier job if the set is co-ordinated in the initial stages to incorporate the lighting. The cost of re-rigging is often expensive and is always time-consuming.

So, for many weeks, the lighting designer will be sitting at a drawing board, working in plan and elevation (a cross-section plot of the stage, showing the height of the set and the lighting equipment). Thus the light designer ensures that whe luminaire is chosen for a job, projection will not be blocked borders or scenery and the li will cover all the area requir It would be ideal if there v also a model of the set to ha

Initially, of course, the light designer must read the sc and analyze it from a light point of view. Then he or s will be ready to discuss production.

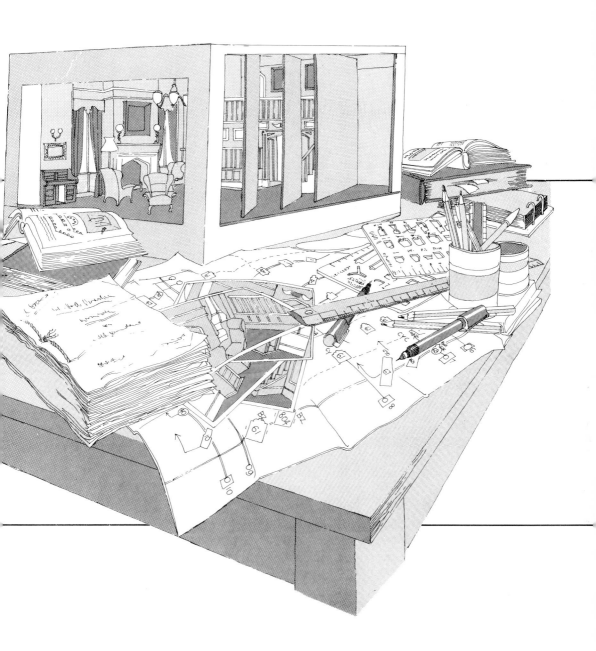

The early stages

Script analysis

The starting point of any production for the lighting designer should be a thorough analysis of the script. Even from a first, brief reading, many ideas will spring to mind. Certainly, the more obvious lighting demands should become clear and these will be the first to note, so jot down all the following information:

The time of day (such as morning, night, dusk, or dawn); the general mood of a scene (such as bright and amusing, or rather sombre and serious); and the more obvious lighting cues (lights being switched on or off, blackouts, and so on):

Exactly how the scene is lit; either artificially, by "practical" lamps — that is a light on the set which actually operates and is not merely decorative; or by natural daylight; or by a totally abstract form of illumination, such as might be used when lighting a musical.

Finally, if a scene is to be lit by artificial light, then record the source, such as electric light, candles, an open fire, gaslight, torches, and so on.

All this basic information is easily accessible from a first reading of a script and will at least give a broad outline of lighting requirements.

To illustrate how to examine a script rather more closely, Professor R.A. Shakespeare of Indiana University has provided the following description of a play, as analyzed by one of his students.

The Zoo Story
by Edward Albee

Zoo Story is a play about two characters, Peter and Jerry, and through them illustrates the desperation of contemporary man. It demonstrates his isolation within the community and his impotence inside the strictures of its culture and the social-economic system.

The characters of Jerry and Peter may often be seen as fragments of one single personality. Their union hardly forms a well-rounded human being but they do create a modern, masculine image.

The play does not offer any real hope; having made desperate attempts to extend beyond himself, to communicate with the outside world, and with Peter in particular, Jerry is killed. Peter is left as a terrorized,

completely wounded charact Their tragedy is unresolved.

These two separate characte and the unstable whole m they occasionally create, m be reflected in the approach the lighting.

To illustrate this concept, Je and Peter should be kept in th own distinct realms of lig having moments when th come close, and only f uniting when Jerry impa himself on the knife Peter holding. Only occasiona should this emphasis be jarring that it is consciou perceived by the audience, the lights must not overshad the characters.

No attempt should be made naturalism; the stage sho not be given the act appearance of Central Park o summer Sunday afternoon.

Cue sheet

owever, the light may move om a color selection of amber nes at the start, to blue and agenta while the play ogresses, culminating in an creasingly disturbed mood at e end of the drama when ese two people are beyond e grasp of the rational. The ht simply cannot have the arm beauty of sunshine and a rk. It is not a pretty play.

rry represents, more often an not, the cruelty of man. He subversive and fierce. Peter, the other hand, represents nat could be considered ndness; he is passive and commodating. Therefore the lges of Jerry's light must quite hard, and hot colors e needed to give clarity to e seething nature of his rsonality. The lighting for ter should be less focused, pressionable, and pastel.

Cue sheet

Note: "Void" means negative space and emptiness

House down to level one to two in 7 count, hold 3 count. House out in 5 count

Q1 page 11
Stage lights up after Peter enters and takes his place on the bench.

SEE: Bench area surrounded in light, therefore separated as an island from the rest of the stage which is void-line. Bench area floor to be textured.

Q2 page 11
SEE: As Jerry enters, island delineation disappears, spreading the texture out across the stage.

Q3 page 12
Jerry: "Mister, I've been to the Zoo."

SEE: As Jerry approaches, stops, yells, island forms again. For the first time we see Jerry sharply focused against Peter's less-defined features.

WHY? This space has opened up to let Jerry in, encapsulating him alone with Peter. Initial contact indicative of their entire encounter — Jerry's aggression to Peter's off-guard reception.

[Follow on]

SEE: Balance in their respective states of brightness as conversational tone is taken.

WHY? So the audience anticipate quickly the intensity of this relationship.

Q4 page 16
Jerry: "But you wanted boys."

SEE: Peter's color change to take on a highlight of the void color.

WHY? Sense the depth of Peter's powerlessness, impotence. Atmosphere: chilly, disquiet.

Q5 page 19
Jerry: (remembering) "Wait until you see the expression on his face."

SEE: Jerry in a cloud of color. Peter returns to normal pastel state.

WHY? Jerry in another world.

Q6 page 20
Jerry: "The Zoo?"

SEE: Jerry return to his previous state.

WHY? Because he has returned to the present.

Q7 page 21
Jerry: "It's one of those things a person has to do...correctly."

SEE: Jerry moves to Area III.

WHY? As he moves the light will come up on an area, falling again once he is no longer there. So illumination bursts into life and then dies — open, then close.

Q8 page 21
Peter: "Oh, I thought you lived in the village."

SEE: Peter's image flattens out.

WHY? Dulled senses.

Cue sheet

Q9 page 24
Jerry: ".... and I have no feeling about any of it that I care to admit to myself."

SEE: Brief dip in Jerry's brightness, Peter less flat.

WHY? Like a sigh, fatigue.

[Return to previous lighting state Q8]

Q10 page 25
Jerry: "I never see the pretty ladies more than once, ...camera."

SEE: Jerry in void shade, slightly redder. Peter no longer flat.

WHY? Cannot sustain, cannot build, brittle, mean.

Q11 page 27
Jerry: But I imagine you'd rather hear about what happened at the Zoo."

SEE: Jerry's previous color comes back, red returning.

WHY? Break, return to first subject.

Q12 page 30
Jerry: "What I mean is animals are indifferent to me...time."

SEE: Jerry's brightness goes up slightly.

WHY? Indifference? Animals?

Q13 page 31
Jerry: "Don't react, Peter; just listen."

SEE: Peter momentarily brought up brighter. Floor starts to lose gobo effect.

WHY? Attention, Self-conscious, flush..."kill?"

[FO Peter's light goes back to old brightness. Jerry in Area I.]

Q14 page 32
Jerry: "People looked up."

SEE: Peter goes slightly dimmer.

WHY? Absorbtion, suggests the adrenalin pulsing!

Q15 page 34
Jerry: "I had tried to love, and I had tried...themselves."

SEE Peter back to normal illumination. Jerry begins to go brighter, color vivid.

WHY? Understanding, realization.

Q16 page 35
Jerry: "I have learned that neither kindness...emotion."

SEE: Full realization of Jerry's light state.

WHY? Clear, bright, hot.

Q17 page 36
(Silence)

SEE: Jerry hollowed, shadow effect as he sits.

WHY? Past his peak, burnt out.

Q18 page 39
Jerry: ".... to find out more about the way people exist with animals,......too."

SEE: Peter growing less muted. Floor texture goes.

WHY? Pressure, surface tension, descend.

Q19 page 43
Peter: "I feel ridiculous."

SEE Void color comes up on Peter, a bit sharper. Rhythm progression, coming together their respective light states.

WHY? Distortion, blows of frustration.

Q20 page 44
Jerry: ".... is this your honor:

SEE: Step 2, both with touch of void color.

WHY? Punctuation, goading.

Q21 page 45
Jerry: "Like a man?"

SEE: Step 3

WHY? Holding

Q22 page 47
(With a rush he charges Peter and impales himself o the knife.)

SEE: Same light, both in Are V. Hollow, sharp, other worl envelops around figures, vo color closing in on island.

WHY? Union, futile.

[FO Moving apart: Peter now hollow and increasingly less focused. Jerry less bright, already becoming wrapped i another world.]

Q23 page 49
Peter off-stage, Jerry on ber Entire stage in void color.

WHY? Frigid pain.

House lights to level one to in 7 count, hold 3. House lig up full in 5 counts.

Solving lighting problems

The discussion stage

All too often, unfortunately, the lighting designer is invited to join the production team's discussions when the set has already been designed and a model of it built — a *fait-compli!*

Therefore, if there are any major problems with lighting the set, it is often too late for the design to accommodate certain lighting requirements.

The lighting designer will then have to solve the problems some other way. There have been a number of productions when a particular lighting position has been impossible to accommodate, and light has had to be bounced off mirrors and back into the set. It is often necessary to compromise, so the sooner the lighting designer becomes involved, the better. All aspects of the production are more readily adjusted in their early stages.

Assuming that the lighting designer has already studied the script, this first meeting will be the next stage in discovering just how the show is going to be. This is usually the time when the model of the set is presented, with or without its inherent problems.

Further discussions with the production team, as well as the director, should soon take place. The ideas of all concerned need to be assimilated, especially the director's vision of the production, until eventually the various concepts will, hopefully, "gel" together. Then the planning of the lighting rig can really start.

Problems to be discussed

Early consultation with the set designer and director will add to the basic information gleaned from the script. With this in mind, and an inspection of the model of the set (this may be just a white cardboard "mock-up" at this stage), various problems may arise.

Awkward areas

The best lighting sites are not always available. For example, when a projector is required, time and again the lighting designer discovers that the set design prevents the projector being accommodated in the ideal position, which can often be the case if the projector is a very large one. A mirror must then be used to reflect the image to the required position. Mirrors are very useful; they often come to the rescue when a lighting position is awkward.

An open (or exposed) rig

A general discussion may take place to decide whether or not the rig should be open (unmasked). If it is open, the design will have no borders and the luminaires will be visible However, with a little ingenuity, the lighting rig can be designed to be incorporated as part of the set and shaped to enhance the overall concept, while still remaining a practical vehicle for the lighting design.

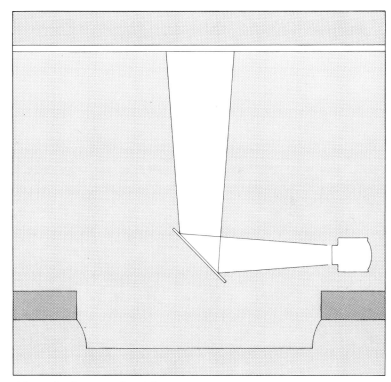

Use of mirror to divert beam

Solving lighting problems

Ceilings

When a lighting designer is first handed the model of a set, two important questions about the design are immediately answered: Is it a box set? Does it have a ceiling?

A ceiling severely restricts the lighting positions available on the stage. It is altogether easier,

from a lighting point of view, if the ceiling is "suggested" rather than a permanent feature. At this point, however, it is not too late for the lighting designer

to ask for a few concessio If it can be masked, a nic might be cut into the ceil piece to accommodate lighting bar.

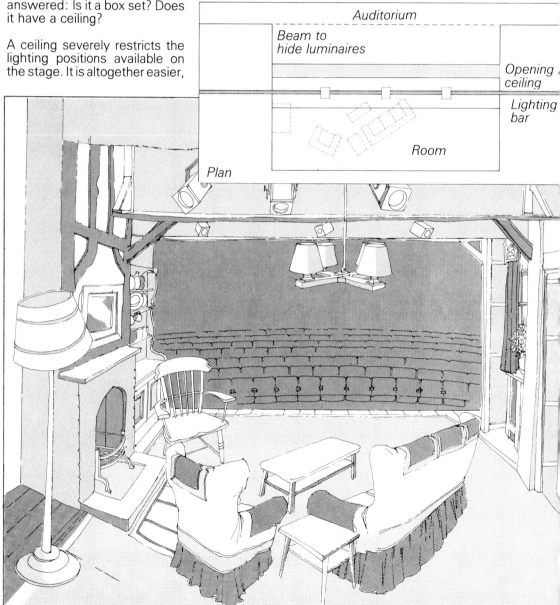

Auditorium

Beam to hide luminaires

Opening ceiling

Lighting bar

Room

Plan

Lighting bar set into niche and masked by ceiling beams

ccomodating side light

e (or cross) light may be sential to a particular lighting t. If this is the case, then the es of the set staging must be e to accomodate all the ders, stands, or booms ich the lighting designer will ed to use.

boom, or light tree, is a tical barrel or pipe, which metimes has "arms", and

which has a heavy base. It is bolted and secured at the side of the stage where it supports luminaires for side lighting.)

The ideal situation in which to place these lights is behind side flats or legs. (Legs are vertical curtains or scenery which are hung to mask the sides of the stage from view.)

Lighting booms or ladders can then be sighted immediately up

stage of these structures. If possible, the masking (whether flats or legs) should be angled so that the on-stage edge is turned very slightly down stage, towards the audience.

At this angle, the masking will create its own shadow and prevent any light which crosses the stage from one side to the other from splodging all over the masking on the opposite side.

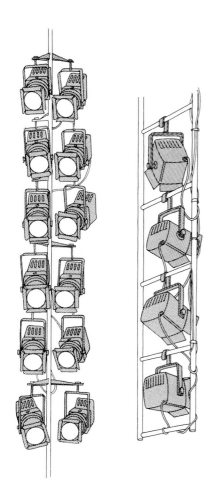

boom or light tree and a lighting ladder

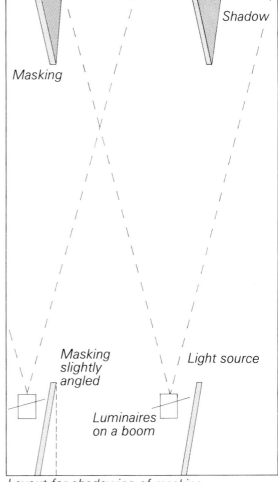

Layout for shadowing of masking

Solving lighting problems

The Cyclorama

The set designer may have chosen to use a wrap-around cyclorama. (This means that the cyclorama is, literally, wrapped around the sides and the back of the stage.)

At first, it might appear to be impossible to incorporate any lighting positions from the side with this arrangement. It is, however, still possible to use side lights with a wrap-around cyclorama, provided this can be "doctored" a little.

The best method is to "tent" the cyclorama. The material at the bottom half of the "cyclorama" is split in a vertical line and separated to form a "tent", behind which lighting booms can be hidden.

A conventional untented wrap-around cyclorama will not permit light to enter the set from the side, whereas a tented wrap-around cyclorama will allow the use of side light. If the tenting is carefully placed, most of the audience will be unaware that it exists.

All these potential problems, which can arise from the particular demands of the production in hand, should be thoroughly investigated and discussions held as soon as possible. Difficulties and conflicts may arise later if these basic problems are not resolved in the early pre-planning stages. Hopefully, the production team will develop an understanding of each other's needs and of the play as a whole.

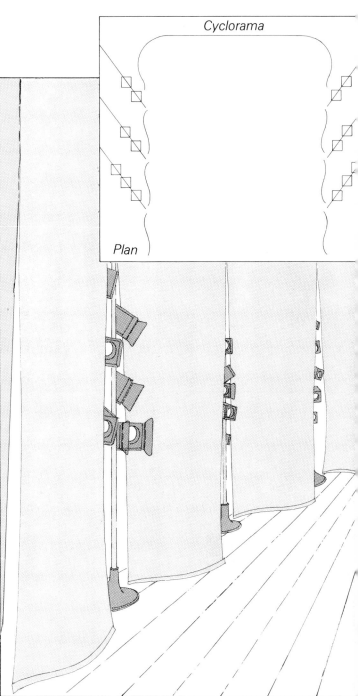

Cyclorama

Plan

A tented cyclorama

The model of the set

The director and the lighting designer should use the early discussion stage to express their views about the set with the designer. Hopefully, any major problems can be resolved at this time. Then, when at last everyone is happy with the basic ideas, a full model of the set will be completed by the set designer to encompass these.

This model will be a much more detailed product than was the first white cardboard "mock-up". It will represent the set and all the scene settings, painted and decorated so that they appear exactly as they will on stage — only in miniature.

When the model is complete, the lighting designer will then have a very clear picture of how the show is going to be staged.

The most widely-used scale is one to twenty-five (1:25). This means that the set will eventually be constructed and painted exactly like the model, only now it will be twenty-five times bigger!

Other scales that may be used:

one to fifty (1:50)
one to twenty (1:20)
quarter inch to one foot ($\frac{1}{4}$":1ft)
half inch to one foot ($\frac{1}{2}$":1ft)

Model of the set for The Gondoliers

The lighting plan

The ground plan

At this point, the set designer may also produce a ground plan. This plan will represent the exact layout and position of the set on the stage, just as the model did but this time in two dimensions. It will be drawn to exactly the same scale as the model was constructed. This will avoid any confusion over measurements and generally makes life easier when it is necessary to look at the model and the plan side by side.

On occasions, the lighting designer may be lucky enough to be given the first choice of lines (line sets) but this is not often the case. Invariably the lighting designer can use only the flying lines that are still available and have not already been allocated elsewhere.

So it is very important to make full use of the early production meetings to discuss the lighting needs with the set designer. Then the lines can be allocated to best suit all concerned. Compromises can be made, such as the moving of a border to facilitate a better lighting position. In this way, the lighting designer should be able to set about the marking up of the ground plan without feeling too restricted and frustrated. His ideas have already been taken into account.

Reproducing lighting structures on paper

There are, of course, various forms of light angles and positions which can be used. These will be referred to as "lighting structures" (see also pages 44-50).

Front light, side or cross light, back light, bottom or up light, top or down light, and silhouette — all these are potential lighting structures.

Each will be selected for its own special characteristics. Very often, a number of different lighting structures will be used together. However, if used in isolation, most structures can be very dramatic; up light is always particularly effective.

Each lighting structure has its own way of being represented on a lighting plan and elevation. It is important to understand how this is done in order to make full use of this early planning stage.

The lighting designer, having explored the possibilities of all the available lighting structures, has to represent them on plans and elevations in this manner. By doing so, all the ideas are properly recorded so they can be readily discussed, and will be planned in an organized way.

Using symbols on the plan

The equipment chosen by the lighting designer will need to be represented on the lighting layout plan. The set designer will normally supply a master plan showing a bird's eye view of the stage.

The layout of the set design will already have been incorporated on to this plan. The lighting

designer's first task is indicate on it the lines of t bars, or pipes, on which all t lighting equipment will be hu in place.

The designer will then enter to these lines a symbol represent each piece equipment that is required. It quite in order to devise personal system for th provided the chosen patter are always drawn to sca consistent, and can be clea understood by means of a ke

Alternatively, stencils can purchased which provide hig accurate representations individual pieces of equipme These are made of bevel plastic and are similar to t stencils used to help studer draw chemistry equipme They are, however, rath expensive, but well worth t outlay as the accuracy of th scale enables the designer judge exactly how each lumi aire will fit the available ar especially important if space at a premium.

If these stencils are beyond yc budget, a good compromise to use a set of symbols that already widely used and v therefore be easily understo by others who may need to lo at the plan.

One such system is illustrat on the right:

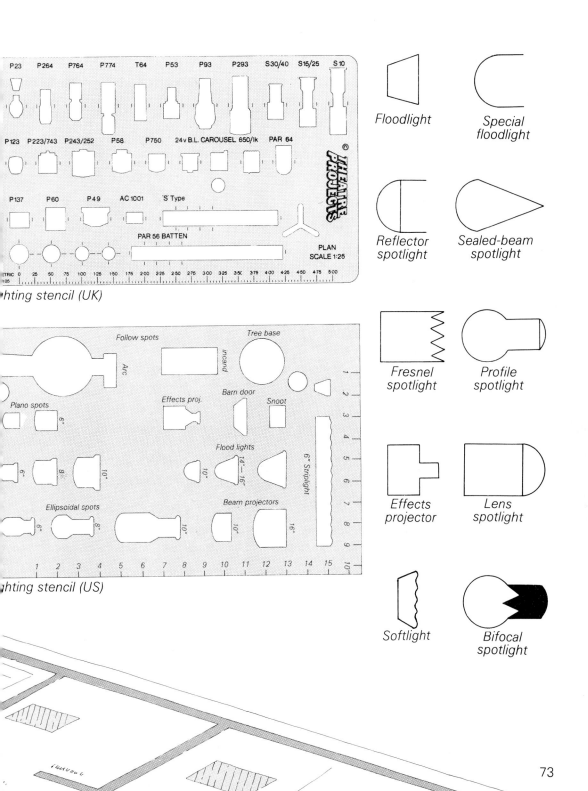

P23 P264 P764 P774 T64 P53 P93 P293 S30/40 S15/25 S10

P123 P223/743 P243/252 P58 P750 24v B.L. CAROUSEL 650/lk PAR 64

THEATRE PROJECTS ®

P137 P60 P49 AC 1001 'S Type

PAR 56 BATTEN

PLAN
SCALE 1:25

METRIC 0 25 50 75 100 125 150 175 200 225 250 275 300 325 350 375 400 425 450 475 500
1:25

...hting stencil (UK)

Follow spots   Tree base

Arc   incand

Plano spots   Effects proj.   Barn door   Snoot

6"

6"   8"   10"   Flood lights   14"—16"   10"   6" Striplight

Ellipsoidal spots   Beam projectors

6"   8"   10"   10"   16"

1 2 3 4 5 6 7 8 9 10 11 12 13 14 15

1 2 3 4 5 6 7 8 9 10

...hting stencil (US)

Floodlight

Special floodlight

Reflector spotlight

Sealed-beam spotlight

Fresnel spotlight

Profile spotlight

Effects projector

Lens spotlight

Softlight

Bifocal spotlight

The lighting design

Further discussion

Before the luminaires can actually be placed on the plan, the lighting designer will probably find that more information is required. The study of the script and the general ideas about the play obtained at the first meeting will now need to be augmented by more serious consultation with the director.

It should not be forgotten that by now the lighting designer will have formulated a far more definite idea of how the play is going to appear to the audience, of its visual impact. So now is the time that the finer points of the design will need to be considered.

If special effects are required, they will almost certainly need to be considered at this time too. This subject is discussed separately in *Special effects* (pages 112-141).

Hopefully, the set designer will also attend this consultation. Using the model to illustrate what is actually happening, the show can be analyzed, scene by scene. Each person has a chance to make suggestions, and the lighting designer should use this opportunity to try and blend all these different ideas into a central design.

Ideally, the design should fulfil all the directorial concept requirements, enhance both the set and the costumes, and also include the lighting designer's own vision of the production. Every show will reflect the work you have contributed and may even bear your own personal "stamp".

At the same time, it must be remembered that the lighting design has to be a team effort. These meetings are essential because the designer cannot work successfully in isolation.

Hopefully, the result of all these consultations will be a unified show — a carefully blended combination of all the elements of production.

The first rehearsal

If possible, the lighting designer should always try to attend the first day of rehearsals. This is when he or she will have an opportunity to hear the play being read through by all the members of the cast.

It is surprising how mu information can be gair simply by listening to the act as they read through the scr Certain moods, that are not a apparent during an isola study of the silent scr suddenly emerge in the spok word. These changes of mc should be noted straight aw because it may be decided accentuate them by means the lighting design.

Planning the rig

By now the lighting desig should be ready to s planning the rig on paper, to t all the ideas and discussic into plots, plans, and elevatio using a set of symbols.

rely will the designer have a
mpletely free choice of
uipment. Instead, it is usually
cessary to work within a
rticular budget or to utilize
ly the theater's own set
minaire stock.

it is absolutely vital to make a
reful choice of equipment
ich can do all that is required
d achieve the desired effect.
w lovely it would be if a
hting designer could always
oose all the luminaires and
uipment he or she would like
st, with a completely free
nd. However, such an ideal
uation seldom occurs!

In any event, whatever the
budget, each piece of lighting
equipment must be selected for
its optical characteristics. This
information is contained in the
chapter on equipment (see
pages 26-51).

How to approach the lighting design

Each lighting designer has his or
her own way of approaching a
new lighting design. Much
depends on the type of
production. For instance, the
way to start work on a musical,
which requires a good many
follow spots, would probably be

quite different from the
approach to a serious drama.

Generally, however, it is best to
start by working out how to light
the acting area. If this is well
covered and lit in a structured
way, so that all the areas of light
can be controlled, you are well
on the way to creating a
technically well-lit show. This
must be achieved first and
foremost. The design element
of the lighting can then be taken
into account.

Choosing the lighting structure

In order to light the acting area (often referred to as AA), many different lighting structures may be used. Careful consideration must be given to the properties of each potential structure and how it might be used in the production (see pages 44-50).

It is possible to combine several structures. Back light and front light might be used together, or front light and side light might make a useful combination. Perhaps the drama of the situation would be better highlighted by a single lighting structure. Down light or bottom light, used alone, may give the required effect. Do not necessarily determine to have the first and most obvious lighting structure which leaps to mind. Do explore all the possibilities.

Dividing the acting area into sections

Once the ground plan has arrived, it is useful to have a means of dividing the acting area into workable proportions. Then each segment of the stage can be allocated its own luminaires, and note taken of whether these are to be used for front light, back light, or whatever structure has been decided upon.

How the stage is to be divided will depend on a number of different factors:

1 The size of the stage
2 The shape of the set
3 The quantity of equipment that is available

All these elements must be taken into account on the lighting plan.

As a general rule, it is usually most convenient to split the stage into nine segments. Divide the acting area by three lines that go across and three lines down. This division of the stage will make a good starting point from which to work out the details of the lighting layout.

Each of these nine sections can now be treated as a little stage in its own right. Each should have its own 45 degree front

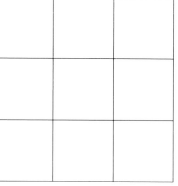

light. Perhaps each might al have its own back light, si light, or down light.

In this way, the lighting of ea area can be carefully control and the illumination of t stage as a whole is far mc manageable. It is then possit to ensure that the acting ar receives good even cover a that the actors are well lit, matter where they move to the stage.

*Divide the stage into suitabl
segments and light each are*

abeling the acting area

fore any decisions can be
en about how to light each of
sections, they must be
en names by which they can
referred to individually,
erwise there will be terrible
ifusion at a later stage.

ch segment should therefore
clearly labeled on the plan.
en every luminaire can be
rked with its appropriate
us point.

e method of labeling each
a is very much a matter of
sonal choice. However, the
ering used in the diagram on
right has much to
ommend it.

the first place it is a very
ical system. Moreover, once
are familiar with it, you will
d that it is very flexible. It can
readily extended and the
erent sections are easily
morized, because they will
hain constant. AX is always
wnstage right; CZ is always
stage left — unless the stage
particularly deep and the
ting designer is required to
oduce a D row.

e common link is that A, B,
d C always go across the
ge, with A at the front; and X,
and Z run up stage, as shown
he diagram opposite.

her methods of labeling will
found. Some are perfectly
od; others are confusing, but
ne can be as flexible as this
t method, once the main
a is committed to memory.

her methods are described
pages 78-79. These will need
be adapted if the stage is an
conventional shape.

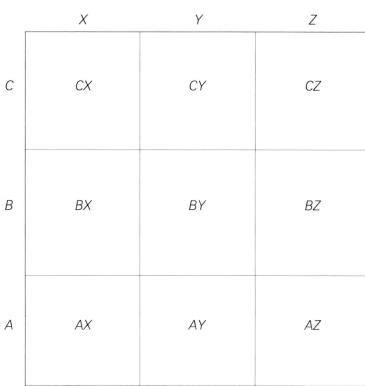

A suitable method of labeling the acting area

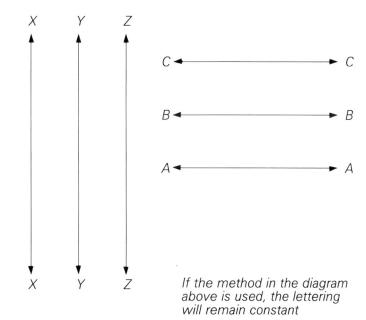

*If the method in the diagram
above is used, the lettering
will remain constant*

Labeling the acting area

1 *This method is most confusing of all as it adds yet another number on to the mark-up of a luminaire. Letters are far more readily recognized, amongst all the other numbers referring to color, circuit, and so on*

7	8	9
4	5	6
1	2	3

2 *This is better than method 1, although still very clumsy and rather time-consuming to write on each luminaire*

VII	VIII	IX
IV	V	VI
I	II	III

This is the best of the
alternatives but it lacks
flexibility if the areas are to be
memorized. (A need not
always be downstage right
or H up center)

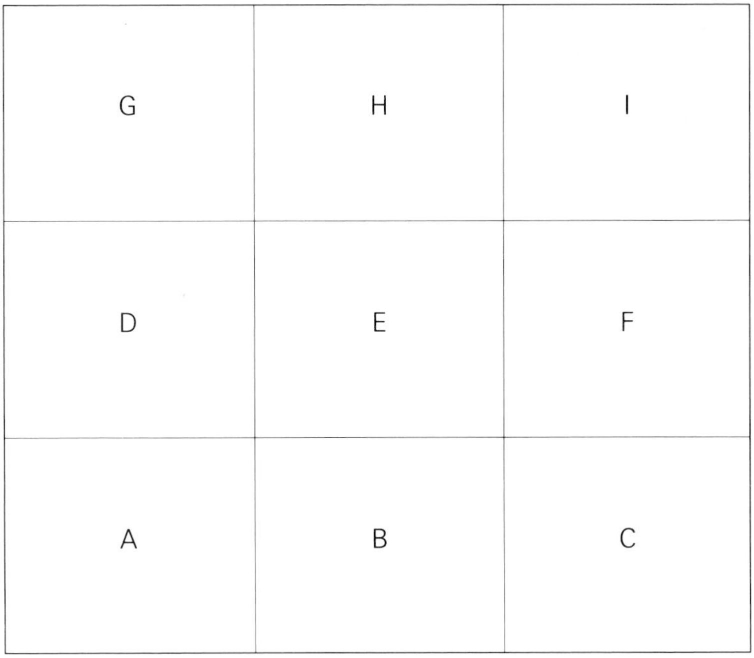

G	H	I
D	E	F
A	B	C

So this last system remains
the best of all. For quick
reference during rehearsal,
when lighting the stage, or
referring to a plan, this
method is definitely the most
useful, once one is familiar
with its logic

CX	CY	CZ
BX	BY	BZ
AX	AY	AZ

79

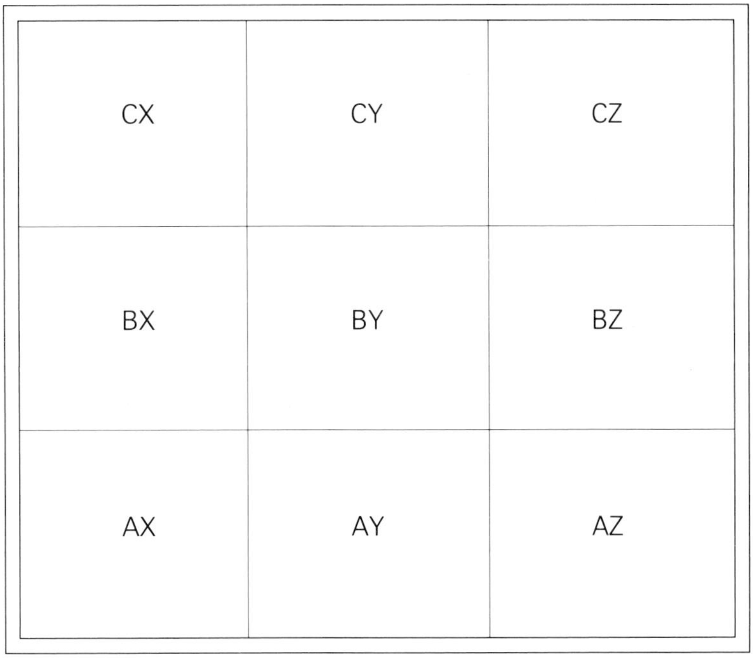

Labeling the acting area

For instance, imagine you are trying to take quick notes during a rehearsal. An actor walks across the stage in the down-stage position. One could write, "Henry V walks across down stage". But, if using method 4, the move is described as, "Henry V walks across A". So less time is required!

Even when the move is a more complicated one, this system simplifies matters. Here is another example: "Mr Waldo moves from up stage center to down stage center" or, "Mr Waldo moves through Y".

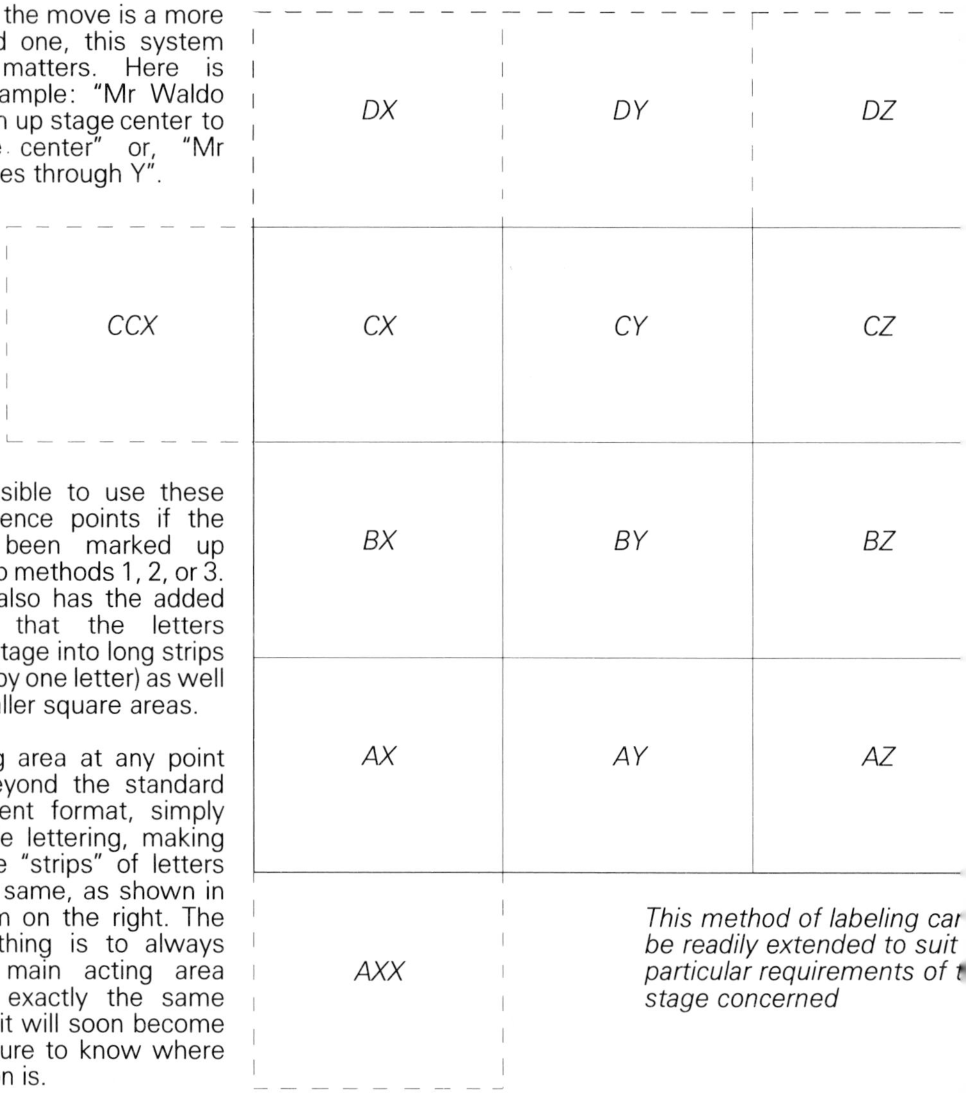

It is impossible to use these quick reference points if the plan has been marked up according to methods 1, 2, or 3. Method 4 also has the added advantage that the letters divide the stage into long strips (described by one letter) as well as into smaller square areas.

If an acting area at any point extends beyond the standard nine-segment format, simply add suitable lettering, making sure all the "strips" of letters remain the same, as shown in the diagram on the right. The important thing is to always keep the main acting area labeled in exactly the same way. Then it will soon become second nature to know where each section is.

	DX	DY	DZ
CCX	CX	CY	CZ
	BX	BY	BZ
	AX	AY	AZ
	AXX		

This method of labeling can be readily extended to suit particular requirements of the stage concerned

ow to make up the lighting eas of a stage is very much up the individual. Experiment th different ideas. A designer ould ultimately choose the ethod that he or she finds ost logical and easiest to use.

ne most important point when viding up an acting area is not make each area so small that e rig becomes too complex. If is happens, merely providing over for the acting area will haust the existing allocation of equipment. There will be no lights left for "specials", scenic effects, or whatever else might be required.

At the same time, the sections should never be too large. Otherwise there will not be enough controllable areas, and the cover from the luminaires lighting each section may be stretched too far.

For example, under normal circumstances, an acting area of twenty-four feet square can be divided into nine segments, each of which is eight feet square. Each of these nine segments is then lit like a little stage in itself.

Always start with the front light. It is this light that will largely light the actor so that he or she can be seen. If possible, each segment should be lit from both sides — at a 45 degree angle to the center, from the horizontal and vertical plane.

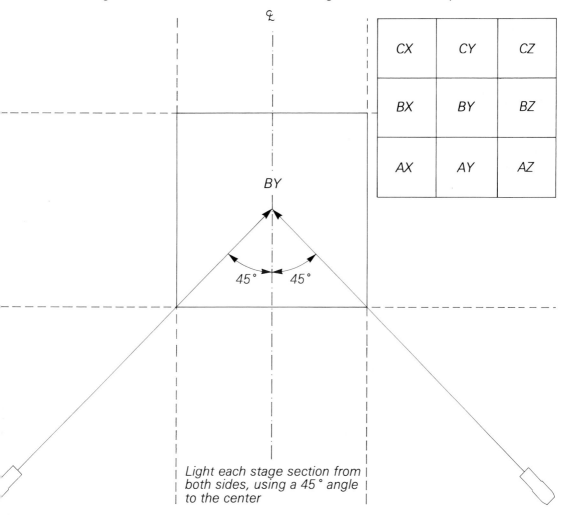

CX	CY	CZ
BX	BY	BZ
AX	AY	AZ

BY

45° 45°

Light each stage section from both sides, using a 45° angle to the center

81

Lighting the stage sections

So, however many segments the acting area has been divided into, each will have two luminaires for front lighting. On a nine-segment area, eighteen luminaires will be used. It is desirable (if space and budget allow) to double this allocation, so that each segment now has two luminaires per side. Thus four front luminaires will be used for each area. Two luminaires should be fitted with a cool tint and two with a warm tint. In this way, both a warm and cool wash can be used.

The temperature of the whole acting area can now be controlled (from warm to cool,

or any state in between) by using both the color washes at varying light-intensity levels. This is obviously far more interesting and adaptable than flat white light.

So the whole acting area is lit, as shown in the small diagram below, by the overall effect of all these individual, controllable lighting areas.

If it is possible to fix each lamp to a different circuit, this effect may be clearly demonstrated. Each portion of the stage can be lit individually, or as a unit of the whole stage, to provide a good wash or cover of light.

The equipment used for th cover light will depend on t preference of the desigr concerned — a choice that v be much easier to make afte careful study of all the availa equipment (see pages 52-59

When lighting through proscenium arch, profiles normally used to project t light through the proscenir arch opening. What happe next depends upon the desi of the current production, bu side or back light is to be add at this point, then the suppos source of the light in the pl must be considered.

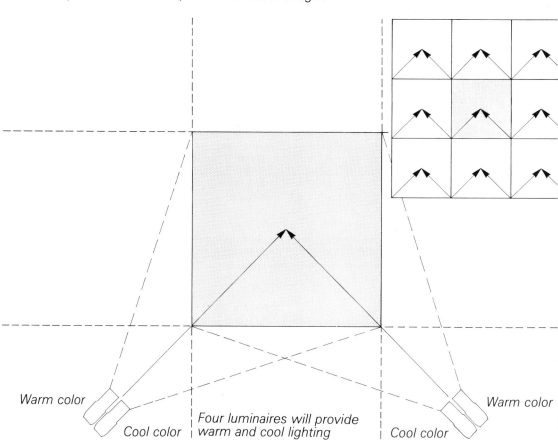

Warm color

Cool color

Warm color

Cool color

Four luminaires will provide warm and cool lighting

Key and fill light

Often the side or back light will provide the "key" light. The key light will be the strongest or most evident direction of light. It will emanate from the most natural point in that particular set — from the direction of whatever source of light is supposed to be there. This could be the moon, the sun, or a standard lamp!

Once the key light is decided upon, any other light on the set will be the fill light.

To further clarify the difference between key and fill light, let us take daylight as an example.

The sun is the light source, so the direction of this light will be the key light. However, we can still see an object or person facing away from the sun. This is possible because of the light which is dispersed or reflected. In a stage situation, this light which is reflected would be recognized as the fill light.

Reflected light may be transmitted from surrounding buildings, from objects, or bounced off the ground; dispersed light comes from the atmosphere and clouds.

So, for instance, try to visualize a box set with a window up stage and daylight outside. One would imagine the room to be lit by the light which is coming through the window.

Fill light (soft)
Key light (hard)

The sun is a source of key light, and reflected light acts as fill light

Key and fill light

The key light, therefore, will come from behind the actor (as though through the window). So, in this case, the back light will be the key light. As this is meant to be daylight, the designer ought to choose equipment which gives a strong hard light source for this back light; perhaps profiles or Pars.

The light bouncing off the room walls will be the fill light. The designer should therefore choose a soft light to use as side light, such as a Fresnel.

Obviously, if the room was lit by artificial light — perhaps by wall-lights set above the fireplace, the key light would then be from this source. So, in the set depicted in the diagram, the key light would be provided by the side light which crosses from stage left to stage right; and the fill light would b the light which crosses fro stage right to stage left (as we as the back light and front ligh

Specials

"Specials" may be added to th plan. A special is a lamp use outside the main acting are cover and which is the because it has a specific job do. Perhaps, for instance, a actor needs to appear to be simply by the light of a candle

Despite splitting the stage in numerous segments, it could b that each section is still too larg and general to give the righ effect. In this case, a lamp cou be used, focused tightly on th area to be lit — just for the specific moment. This ligh would be called a special.

Hopefully by now it can be see how the lighting plan may b constructed in an organize way, by working in stages s that nothing is forgotten. All th relevant parts of the stage w have been "covered" wit whatever lighting structure ha been chosen. It may be helpf to work through the plan in logical way, as shown:

1 Front light
2 Key light
(side, back, or top light)
3 Fill light
(side, back, or top light)
4 Add specials
5 Add color
6 Draw on special effects
7 Circuit plan

However do not plan on element of the design isolation. Always keep in min the overall effect so that eac

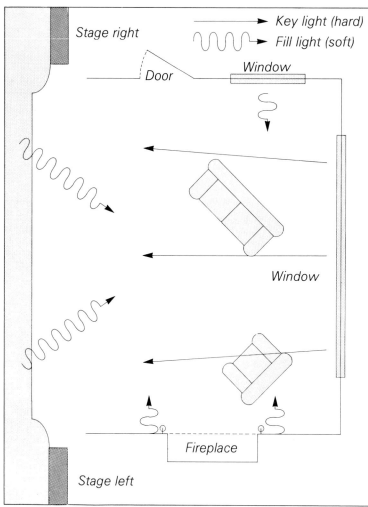

Key and fill light on a typical box set

ment works with and implements the rest. Also do remember the scale of the operation, just what equipment how much is available, how many circuits are available and even, in some cases, how much power. It is so frustrating to draw the ideal plan and then have to "butcher" it because there is more equipment on the plan than is actually available.

As a rule, the plan is first drawn in pencil. A lot of paper planning is done long before the lighting designer can see a complete "run" of the show, (a rehearsal of the show from start to finish).

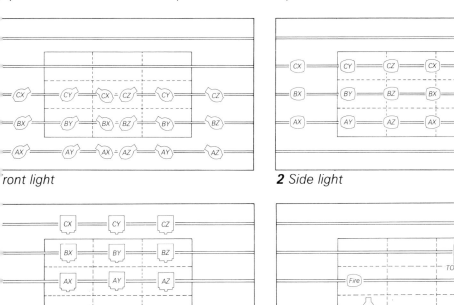

ront light

2 Side light

3ack light

4 Specials

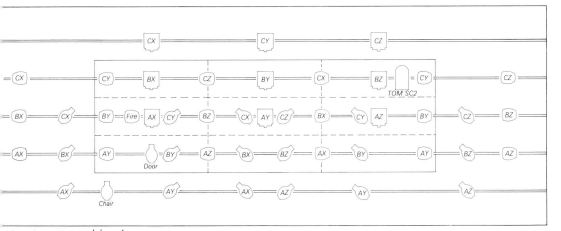

structures combined

Final decisions

After seeing a "run", the lighting designer may wish to make some refinements to the lighting plan; perhaps adding or moving a few specials, or altering color to reflect a certain mood. When the last run is over, the lighting designer and director will meet once more and finalize the cueing notes. Only when the lighting designer is completely satisfied with the plan, will it be finalized and several duplicates made. It is worth remembering that many people will need a copy of the plan — the "riggers" and the electricians, the flyman (so the weight of each lighting bar can be assessed), the technical or stage director and, of course, a clean copy will also be needed for the lighting session — the moment of truth!

When all the luminaires have been allocated to the plan, each one must be clearly marked to indicate its type, its color reference number, its circuit

number, and its focus point. In the USA, an instrument and patch number would be shown.

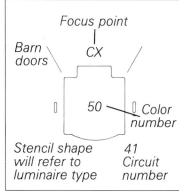

Marked-up luminaire

With experience the lighting designer will know, more or less, what a certain luminaire with a specific beam angle or angles will cover on stage; that is the amount of area it will light, given a specific throw distance. However there are times when even experienced designers

may find themselves relying instinct or guesswork.

On such occasions it is bes do a quick calculation, to m sure the equipment used cover the area required. For a plan and elevation of the will be needed. The beam ar of the luminaire in question the distance of the lumin from the area it is to light throw) must be known.

Then a simple line diagram the same scale as the plan elevation, can be drawn used to calculate the bea cover size. A protractor wil required. Use this to meas the angle required along length of the throw.

The example here (drawn 1:25 scale) shows a 30 deg beam angle luminaire lightir distance of 21.5 meters. It be shown by the calculation the amount of area covered the light will be 1.27 met

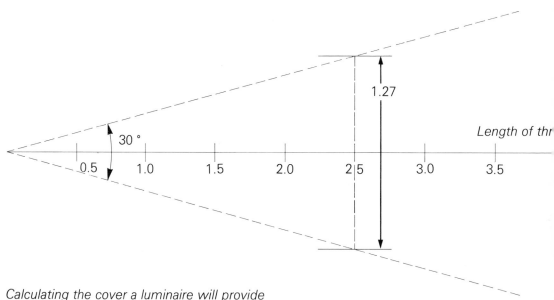

Calculating the cover a luminaire will provide

The thrust stage

So far, we have mainly considered the lighting of a proscenium stage, or at least a staging area where all the audience are sitting in front of the staging area. We should now take into account that not all productions and theaters are quite so conventional.

What considerations should be made when lighting the thrust stage, or for lighting a theater in the round (an arena stage), with an audience on all sides?

When a thrust stage is used, some of the audience will be viewing part of the staging area from the side. If the thrust stage is especially deep, the lighting designer should then consider whether the side of the thrust should be lit as though it were the front — or in the same way as the "real" front. Thus it could be said that a thrust stage has three fronts!

If this option is chosen, the side light for this area will also act as front light for some of the audience, and so this must be taken into account. Most certainly, in these cases, side light is essential to allow actors to be seen when facing stage left or right.

It may be argued that lights should be placed at a 45 degree angle to frontlight the side of a thrust stage. However, the problem is that this light would then interfere with the back light (as shown in diagram A).

Instead, it is best to use a flat front light which comes straight in from the horizontal plane to the side of the thrust stage. This is quite adequate and, in most cases, will look rather better anyway.

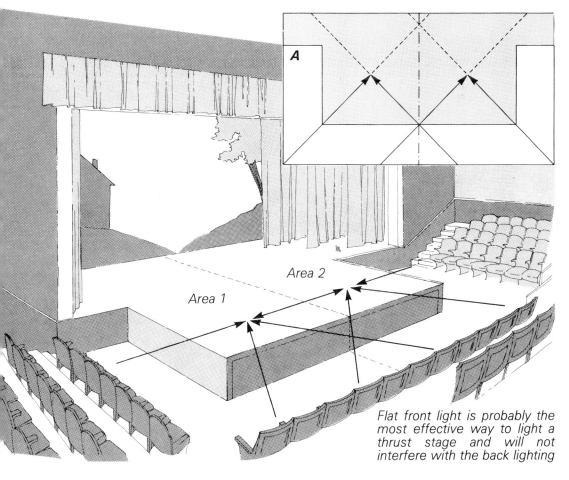

Flat front light is probably the most effective way to light a thrust stage and will not interfere with the back lighting

Lighting in the round (arena stage)

When lighting a theater in the round, it must be remembered that some lighting structures previously dealt with no longer exist in a normal form. This is due to the fact that there is now an audience on every side, 360 degrees around the stage.

The structures therefore take on a different form, depending on where one is sitting around the stage. These changes affect front light, side light, cross light, back light, and silhouette — this last being almost impossible.

It can be seen from the diagram that the people sitting in block A will interpret the lighting structures quite differently to those sitting in blocks B, C, and D. The audience in each block of seats sees the lighting from a different angle.

Take, for example one light source coming into the stage from the front (on the plan).

For those people sitting in block A, this light source is front light; for those in B and D, however, the light becomes side light;

while for those in block C, 1 same light source becom back light. So, in theater in t round, the creation of go acting-area cover means th the front, side, and back li become as one unit — 1 apparent structure of which v depend totally on the angle fro which it is viewed.

When lighting in the round, t initial approach to the provis of acting-area cover is much 1 same as for a conventio stage. The stage must first split into areas.

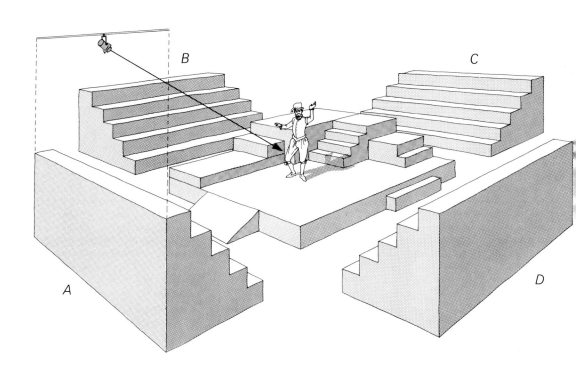

The audience in each block of seats will see the lighting from a different angle

most obvious way of ▪ting each area would be to ▪ng each luminaire at a 45 ▪ree angle to each of the four ▪wing "fronts", as shown in ▪ first diagram below.

▪nting all nine segments like ▪ would indeed give an ▪ellent acting-area cover. By ▪bling the luminaires for each ▪a (using two for each lighting ▪ition), a warm and a cool ▪sh could be provided, as ▪scribed earlier.

▪wever, this method is ▪iously a rather extravagant ▪ and may quickly consume ▪the allocation of equipment. ▪ht luminaires will be needed ▪each area so nine segments ▪uire seventy-two luminaires.

▪quipment budgeting renders ▪ method impracticable, use ▪vider-angled separation of ▪ lights, setting them 120 ▪rees apart. In this way, three ▪inaires instead of four may ▪used to light each segment. ▪doubling up is required, six ▪inaires will be sufficient, and ▪/-four would cover all nine ▪ments of the stage.

This second method reduces The number of luminaires needed to provide the acting-area cover and yet still provides a perfectly adequate and adaptable lighting system.

If coloring the stage is required, but it is not desirable to dramatically color the actor's face, then top light must be considered. This is one of the few lighting structures that will remain constant from whichever point the stage is viewed. To make top light available in each segment would be ideal, and greatly enhance all the sculpturing qualities of the design.

If possible, when a designer is lighting a show, he or she should arrange to see a "run" from each viewing point. This will ensure that, when lighting from any chosen point, the light from the opposite side has not been overlooked.

It may, in fact, be advisable to pair up opposite luminaires. Then, when called upon to light an area from one side, the complimentary luminaire on the opposite side, which is to cover the same area, is automatically illuminated.

Hopefully this literally "new angle" on stage lighting will work well and the challenge of different surroundings will teach all those involved, including the lighting designer, a great deal. He or she may well collect a few new and useful ideas that can be applied to the conventional stage. It is all too easy to become stale if every play is undemanding.

In any event, whatever the shape of the stage or wherever the audience sit, the lighting designer should always try to remember the objectives — that is to reveal the actors, using the lights on the stage to create a temporary world around them. Whether it is moonlight slanting in through an attic window, midday in the Sahara desert, or "special" Christmas-tree lights on a darkened stage, the lighting should be a vital link between the actors, the environment created around them, and the audience who have come to watch.

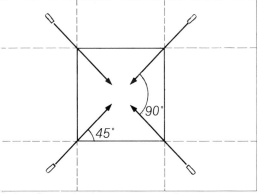

▪hting for a single segment using ▪0 degree separation

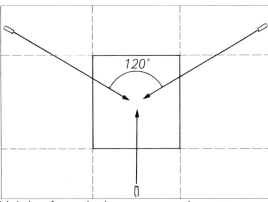

Lighting for a single segment using a 120 degree separation

Production procedure

At this stage of a production, good organization is the most important element. It is now that the designer will reap the benefits of a well-planned and fully prepared lighting scheme. At last all the ideas will come to fruition — but this will be achieved only if preceded by thorough ground work.

This procedure is analyzed mainly from the mechanical point of view, especially in its initial stages, as it is most important to understand the technicalities involved.

Once the lighting rig is safely in position and every luminaire is correctly angled, then the focusing can begin. At this point, the designer will be busy directing operations, and will continue to do so through the lighting session and rehearsals.

When the final dress rehearsal comes to an end, the task of the lighting designer will be largely over until the next show. (This does not apply, of course, to the lighting designer of a small company who is also the operator during a performance.) Lighting may need to be changed occasionally during production; the timing of the play may alter, or the director might decide to change some part of it. Luminaires may move slightly or need readjustment.

Generally though, apart from perhaps the supervision of the rig's removal, the designer can switch attention to the n€ production or to whatever e is "in the pipeline".

During the production schedu the lighting will gradually ha evolved and taken shape. T symbols on the plan will ha been replaced by luminair€ and the ideas in the lighti designer's mind will, hopefu have been realized on the sta¢ The whole production team v have been working very hard this stage, in order to see t final culmination of their effor If all this has been achiev with co-operation and mutı understanding, they will enjoy a well-deserved glow success when they finally s their particular talents blend together into live theater.

Pre-planning

The lighting plan (lighting plot)

The completed lighting plan is the lighting designer's main means of communication at this stage. It is through this plan that all the lighting requirements are made known to the rest of the production team. (Exactly how to compile one is described on pages 72-3.)

Make sure the plan has properly covered every necessary detail; then have sufficient copies of this duplicated to enable every member of the electrics team to have one each. The other production departments will also require a copy and one must be made available for the lighting session. Make sure that these are all distributed in good time (but not so early that they can be forgotten or mislaid!)

Color

If new color filters are needed, purchase these well in advance of the "fit-up". In this way, if there are any problems in obtaining the particular type required, there will still be plenty of time to find an alternative or a different source.

If the budget allows, buy more than just the minimum number required; then you will not be compromised during the fit-up, if it turns out that more gels are required than anticipated.

Look at the lighting plan and draw up a list of the colors that will need to be cut to luminaire size. These can be classified under luminaire size, or according to the position for which they are intended. The second method is probably the

best because it is easier to find the necessary piece when that particular part of the rig is being constructed.

Store all the required colors in a separate envelope for each location. Clearly label every envelope and then there will be no frantic searching later.

Hire of equipment

Any equipment to be hired must be ordered in good time and then carefully checked when it arrives. Make sure it is all in perfect working order and is exactly what is needed. Some pieces of equipment must have special cable so, if this is the case, do check that this has been supplied too and meets your requirements.

Most rental companies enclose a spare lamp with their equipment. Ensure that this is sound — and if it does have to be used during the course of the production, remember to keep the "blown" lamp in a safe place. This will act as proof that this has actually happened. Failure to produce the old lamp could result in an unwelcome extra bill for its replacement.

Cables and adapters

Study the plan once again — this time to count the number of times that pairing occurs.(This is when more than one luminaire is using a single dimmer, as described on page 147.)

Ensure that there are enough adapters ("two-fers") available for all the pairing to be done and that there is enough cable available to feed each luminaire. Always check you are using the

correct size cable for the loa This is particularly importa when the venue is previous unknown to you. If working ir foreign country, all the electric equipment will have to con under close scrutiny to ma sure local regulations a complied with and safe standards are met.

Fuses and spare lamps

During the fit-up and t subsequent removal of the (derig), the luminaires will ha to be moved about so they a more liable to damage than any other time. Handle them carefully as possible. This the most likely time for lam to "blow", especially if t electricians are at all rough w the luminaires. It is therefo wise to keep a stock of lam and fuses in case they a ever needed.

The electrical team

The electricians and riggers w be working very hard to rig th lighting in the time allowe usually under quite difficu circumstances.

In professional theater, th management cannot allo much time between show because money is lost when th theater is closed. So the quick the better!

In amateur productions th pressure may not be so great the company own their ow theater, but often as not, the h: is used by other groups societies and it may not b available until the very la minute. Neither profession nor amateur can afford to boo an empty theater for too long means that time is very cious. Not only will the ting crew be working inst the clock, but the set too probably have to be structed and completed in a rt space of time. Stage nagement, carpenters, and props department will all be y. The actors, as well, will nt to use this opportunity rehearse ' in the new ronment — so there is often npetition for stage space and over-riding sense of panic!

ch depends on how well nized the production is as a ple. It is up to the lighting gner to ensure that his or particular department is in er. If everything has been efully planned, then the tricians will know exactly nt is expected of them and, pite probably having to work hours, will be prepared to their weight" — provided are confident that there is nod in the madness and their needs have been sidered.

ay be a good idea to work a timetable beforehand. lyze the lighting plan and e down just what has to accomplished in the time lable. Try to be realistic in allotment of time and ember to allow for a few l-earned tea-breaks!

not try to win the co-ration of the electrical team large quantities of alcohol here will probably be some ler climbing ahead!

e fit-up is going to involve a d deal of ladder work, it is t to have a minimum of three ple on the team. One person

will climb the ladder, another holds it steady, and the third will be able to pass up the luminaires as required.

Focusing is best done by a team of four. Once again, the first person (who will need to have two strong arms and a head for heights) scales the ladder, ready to focus the luminaires. The second person steadies the ladder, the third puts the circuits

up on the lighting board, and the lighting designer must direct the proceedings to make sure the focusing is accurate.

It is important to allow sufficient time to focus correctly. Any mistakes made at this session will have to be rectified later and may well add to the frustrations of a future lighting session or rehearsal. Allow an average of three minutes per luminaire.

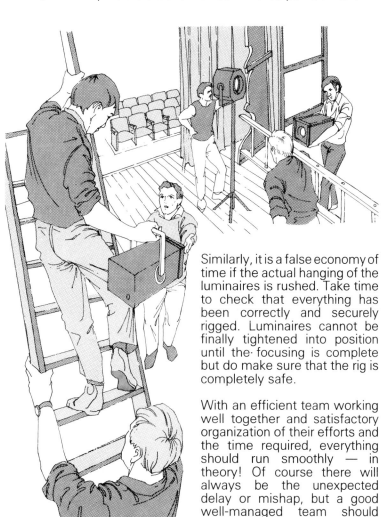

Similarly, it is a false economy of time if the actual hanging of the luminaires is rushed. Take time to check that everything has been correctly and securely rigged. Luminaires cannot be finally tightened into position until the focusing is complete but do make sure that the rig is completely safe.

With an efficient team working well together and satisfactory organization of their efforts and the time required, everything should run smoothly — in theory! Of course there will always be the unexpected delay or mishap, but a good well-managed team should take this in their stride.

The fit-up

Safety

There are invariably other people working on the stage simultaneously with the lighting team. It is sensible therefore to ensure that your work does not impede that of others. Hopefully they will respond by showing some consideration for your needs. Of course this is not always the case and, if another group of people are less well organized, this may lead to short tempers and short cuts. The theater at this time has all the dangers of a building site and great care must be taken to avoid accidents.

This is especially important when scenery is in transit and if there are counterweighted flying bars (or pipes) being rigged. It is vital to be aware of people working above, and below. It is always possible that a heavy object could be dropped. A shout of, "Heads!" is pointless if there is no reaction from the people below.

The safety of the mechanical and electrical equipment is always important. Check and double-check every fitting. Make sure all the nuts are adequately tightened. Don't leave equipment lying around. Make sure plugs are wired correctly and properly inserted into their sockets. Any loose cable must be securely taped to the bars. If any ropes are used, make sure these are sound and are safely anchored. Don't balance ladders on uneven floors. Be especially cautious if the rig is a particularly high one. Scaffolding, or a Tallescope, may have to be used, or even, in extreme situations, a "bosun's chair". Any such operation

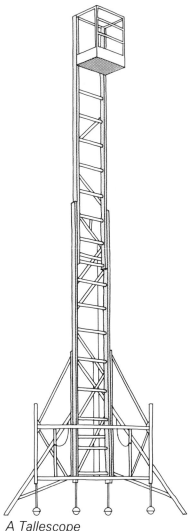

A Tallescope

requires a particular awareness of the inherent dangers.

In any event, great care and discipline must be exercised throughout this stage of the production.

Removing the rig

Occasionally an existing rig may bear a close resemblance to the design of the new rig about to be put into operation. In this case, it will obviously be in y interests to adjust it accordir rather than to totally disma it. In normal circumstanc however, if a rig is still position from the previ production, it will be necess to remove this, and start afre

Begin by unplugging all cables from the dimmers. T unplug and remove them fr the lighting bar (or batte Carefully coil and tape cable

Never try to coil the ca between your elbow and y hand as this twists the v cores and will strain th unnecessarily. Instead it is b to coil the cable by holding it behind the plug or socket in hand, and then use the ot hand to make large loops (ab one meter). Twist the cable you do this so that it ha properly without any kinks i Once the cable has b carefully coiled, it can then taped at one end to kee neatly in shape.

The next job is to remove all luminaires' color frames. W this has been done, close all barn doors and shutters prevent their being damage

If the rig is on a flying syste the counterweights must a unloaded before any lumina are removed from the bar. remove any equipment at from a fully counterweigh bar could be very dangerc Counterweights are extren heavy and their sheer we could cause the bar to fly risking life and limb, possibly damaging the build Should an electrician be foc enough to start work on counterweighted bar, there

ry chance of flying out with it
adding to the spectacle!
ver ever take this risk.

ce the weights have been
oaded, then the luminaires
be safely removed and the
t lighting bar derigged.

e rig is on fixed bars, then it
y be necessary to use a
escope or a rung ladder,
nembering to take all the
essary precautions. It is
netimes very useful to use a
e carefully hung over the
ting bar (or pipe) so that
luminaires can be gently
ered to the person waiting
vn below.

ce all the previous rig has
en carefully removed and
vanted equipment carefully
red away, then the new fit-
can begin in earnest.

gging

e lighting bar will have to be
jed at a time. Having worked
in what order the hanging
uld be done (perhaps to fit
with the set construction),
t gather all the necessary
ipment together and keep it
a convenient place. Make
e everything that you need is
dy before you start.

ce the first luminaire on the
ting bar as indicated on the
ting plan. Angle it so it is
nting in approximately the
t direction. Although this is
y a rough position, it will help,
later stage, to speed up the
using session. Tighten the
k clamp and attach the
ety chain to the bar, leaving
ficient "slack" to allow
vement of the luminaire to
angle.

Continue to rig all the other
luminaires on to the bar, making
sure that each one has
sufficient space around it. The
luminaires must be able to be
adjusted during the focusing
session without "fouling" each
other. Provided the plan has
been drawn up properly to
scale, there should be no such
problems to contend with.

Continue in this way on the next
bar. A methodical "plan of
campaign" will reap dividends
at this time.

Once all the luminaires have
been rigged up according to the
lighting plan, make sure all
the necessary colors and
accessories have been fitted
and that every luminaire has
been allocated a lamp!

Spot bars (or pipes)

If an internally-wired spot bar is
to be used, start plugging the
luminaires into this. Always
begin plugging in at the
opposite end of the bar to the
cable or "tripe" feed. In this way,
should any extra "ways" have to
be inserted later, then shorter
cable lengths can be used.
There will be no need for cable
to travel the full length of the bar
to reach each luminaire.

Tie the socket of the extension
cable around the bar, next to the
luminaire it is feeding. Then
tape it along the bar at intervals
so it remains neatly in place.

Keep "luminaire tail" loose so
that the luminaire can move
without pulling on the cable.
Where a cable leaves the end of
a spot bar, tape it to the end of
this to avoid placing any strain
on the plugs and sockets.

Label and check

The next step in the rigging
session is to make sure that
everything is clearly labeled and
working properly. It is important
to do this efficiently, both for
safety reasons and to ensure
a smooth-running production
schedule. First "flash" through
the rigged bar to test the
offstage ends of the feed cables
and mark them with the circuit
number. Then label the plugs
coming off the spot bar with
their correct circuit numbers.

At the same time, check that
everything is working properly.
Each plug must be inserted into
a working socket. Do this one
plug at a time, and as each
luminaire is lit, check it against
the lighting plan and write the
circuit number clearly on the
plug top. Use large lettering on
adhesive tape so it can be easily
seen, even in the dark.

If any luminaire fails to light, first
unplug it and then make a visual
check to see if the lamp's
filament is still intact. If the lamp
has blown, simply replace it.
Should the lamp appear to be in
working order, try plugging the
luminaire into another cable and
working socket. If it now proves
operational, this means the
cable may be faulty or there is a
loose connection in the plug or
the socket.

Try to correct all such faults well
ahead of the focusing session. It
is far easier to be able to work
through the problems now,
when they can be dealt with
at ground level, than to be
struggling up ladders later when
everything is in its final position.
Never work on any equipment
that is still plugged in.

Focusing

Once all the lighting bars have been rigged and checked, and when everything has been labeled, the bars can then be plugged into their circuits.

To complete the operation, make a final check through all the rig, circuit by circuit, using the lighting board. Double-check that all the plugging and colors used are correct and that every piece of equipment is in working order.

It may not be possible to rig every single piece of equipment at this stage if the set is still under construction.

Some side lighting (such as booms or tormentors) and practical lamps on the stage set itself, or lights that are actually attached to scenery, may have to wait until slightly later. If this is the case, make sure that all the necessary equipment is prepared and fully organized.

Exercise the same methodical check and double-check when their rigging is finally finished, and do not be hustled into overlooking any aspect of this important operation.

Thus, rigging a normal lighting bar may be undertaken safely and successfully if the following routine is carefully observed:

1. Postion the luminaires on the bar, remembering to tighten the hook clamps and to fix the safety chains.

2. Plug luminaires to internally-wired spot bars and to all the extension cables.

3. Open all shutters, barn doors, and color luminaires.

4. "Flash" through the tripe ends and mark all plugs with their correct circuit numbers.

5. Plug the marked tripe ends into the circuit board or patch panel as appropriate.

Focusing

Focusing is, perhaps, the most important part of production procedure.

Each part is, of course, a vital element in its own right and must be executed efficiently, but to achieve really good lighting, and fulfil the realization of the lighting designer's perception of the play, a successful focusing session is absolutely essential.

Ideally, four people will be needed to focus quickly and safely. The lighting designer will stay at stage-floor level and give the directions from there. The electricican will focus the luminaires, according to these directions, from his or her position at the top of the ladder. The third person will be the control-board operator who brings up the circuits; and the fourth person is the one who foots the bottom of the ladder.

There are two ways to focus. The first possible method is to stand with one's back to the luminaire concerned, in order to avoid being blinded by the light. Then direct the electrician to center the luminaire on to the back of your head and judge its position by the effect of the heat on the back of the neck. This is not altogether satisfactory as it is difficult to be accurate without actually looking at the equipment being adjusted.

The second (and rather m efficient) method is to adjust luminaire's light intensity t low level so that it can be loo at comfortably. It is much ea to center the luminaire now you can see the position of filament in relation to reflector. Once the lumin has been centered to y satisfaction, the light can brought up to full and its ef on the scenery, and so properly ascertained.

As each luminaire is focus make sure that it is able provide sufficient cover for particular area that it has b allocated — check that ev part of it is lit. If the a concerned is an acting a ensure that the light overl the divisions slightly. Then actors will be lit comple evenly as they cross from area to another. Test this walking around the appropr parts of the stage with relevant luminaires lit as t will be during the play.

Remember throughout all the actors' actual positions the stage. They may be ly down or sitting on a low c and this must be considere

If a beam hits part of scenery, try to disguise edges of the beam by softer them slightly or aiming th towards the tops of doorwa picture rails, or whatever pa the set is convenient! careful, also, to avoid unwan shadows or hot spots. (stage luminaires (or those behind a backing) might ca problems in this way, especi when an actor is waiting in wings. Try to visualize exactly where everyone will

other problem that might ... attention is spill or ghost ... As each luminaire is ... used and set, do check ... roughly that no unwanted ... kage of light appears on the ... scenium or any borders, ... nery, or backcloth. Have a ... ck glance around the whole ... before you move on to the ... xt light. It is so much simpler ... eradicate at this stage than ... en several luminaires are ... rking together and the "guilty ... ty" is not quite so easily ... ognized.

...e focusing team

...roughout the operation, the ...r members of the lighting ...m who are working together ...ve their separate but co-...inated roles to play.

...e lighting designer

...e lighting designer carries the ...mate responsibility for the ...erall success of the focusing ...ssion. Speed is usually ...sential but accuracy is equally ...portant. Every luminaire must ... literally "spot on"! A few ...hes difference really does ...tter, so do check every ...inaire properly.

...member that the lamps heat ...very quickly, so don't call up a ...ninaire until the electrician is ...dy for it. Then stand in the ...ter of area to be lit and use ...e of the methods already ...scribed to center the ...ninaire to head height.

...ce this has been achieved, ...p out of the beam and adjust ... size to cover the appropriate ...a. Check that this has been ...mpletely lit by walking the ...a. Finally, adjust the barn

doors and shutters to remove unwanted light, and double-check that everything is in order. Carry in your mind clearly the exact function of each luminaire and make sure this is properly achieved.

The electrician

The electrician must first ensure that he or she is in a safe and comfortable position and that all the luminaires are within reach. The next step is to check that all the shutters and barn doors are open and that any Fresnel luminaires are adjusted so that their beams are "spotted down" to the smallest possible beam angle. This will make it easier to center them properly. Make sure that all necessary tools are readily to hand.

Once this has all been done, the electrician should inform the lighting designer that focusing can begin. The designer will then call up the circuit and give instructions as the focusing proceeds. The electrician must follow directions and, as each angle is finalized, lock it into position and tighten all the nuts.

The electrician will be able to see the stage well from the top of the ladder and perhaps is better placed than the rest of the team to check exactly what the light beam is doing. Therefore it can often be helpful to the lighting designer if the electrician makes sure that, from his or her viewpoint too, there are no apparent problems.

Before leaving one focused luminaire for another, double-check that it is securely locked off and will not slide out of position at a later stage.

The speed and efficiency of the operation largely depends on the quality of the electrician!

The board operator

The board operator is the one who is most familiar with all the controls, especially if the board is a very complicated one. He or she is also the most remote member of the team, probably being at some distance from the core of activity but, like the electrician, it will be necessary to follow instructions promptly and to co-ordinate with the rest of the team. Communications between them all may range from shouting, and using a system of signals, to an intercom arrangement. Check that any intercom or telephone system is working properly before focusing begins.

Unless the lighting designer gives instructions otherwise, it is usual to bring up just one circuit at a time. So, when a circuit is requested, put it into effect; then remove any other circuits already being tested.

The ladder crew

The ladder crew, albeit often only one person, must always see that the safety of the operation is ensured. The ladder must be held firmly and then moved as required. Again, it is imperative that all instructions are followed precisely.

The lighting rehearsal

The aim of this first lighting session is to see for the first time on stage an idea of how all the lighting will look, cue by cue. It will not yet be perfect — this first session will be more like a

97

Rehearsals

rough sketch than a detailed drawing, but, if the focusing has been carefully executed, the desired effects should all be there, ready to be molded into their final form when set and actors have all been absorbed into the pattern.

With the focusing complete and the rig all ready, the lighting designer should also be fully prepared for this session.

It is best to view the lighting from a position about halfway down the auditorium. This will usually ensure a balanced lighting state, neither too dark from the back of the auditorium nor too bright near to the stage. (It will be necessary at later rehearsals to check the lighting from other positions, to see that it is correct from every seat in the house.)

Having chosen a good site, ensure that you have everything you need ready, preferably on a desk or table so that script, plots, and the lighting plan can be spread out before you. Do make certain it is possible to communicate with everyone concerned from this vantage point, most especially with the electricians.

A low-level light may be a useful addition to the paraphernalia now doubtless littering an already crowded desk.

A "walker" will need to move about on the stage, aping the actors, to enable the effects of the lighting to be judged effectively. Make sure that someone is ready to take on this task. To light the actors so they can be seen is the prime object of the exercise and this cannot

be assessed on an empty stage. When everything the designer needs is ready and all the lighting team have announced that they, also, are fully organized, the lighting session can begin.

It is best to commence with the house in darkness (allowing for any exit lights or orchestra cover), and then to gradually introduce the required lighting composition for each cue. Begin with the main light source or the key light. For instance, light emanating from a window or doorway, or the daylight slowly filling a cyclorama, should be brought up to its required level before the overall cover lighting is introduced.

It is normal practice to begin at the beginning and then to follow the cue synopsis through to the end. This allows everyone to see the lighting patterns as part of the overall scheme and to evaluate their effects within the context of the whole.

However, this means that if there are any doubts about a particular piece of equipment or effect, it will be necessary to check this beforehand. In fact, a quick test of every circuit before the session begins in earnest may eliminate any later irritating interruptions to the run-through.

As each lighting state is composed on the stage and evaluated with the assistance of the "walker", it must be labeled with a cue number. If both lighting designer and director are happy with the result, it can then be plotted on the lighting board. Never rush this stage. Careful plotting of circuits is vital. A mistake now

could alter the intended eff of the lighting, or even tot ruin a composition.

It is often wise not to take lighting circuits up to full at t initial stage, even for a v sunny scene. The director m well ask for more light and i most frustrating if you ha already exhausted all y reserves. Always keep a li extra light "in stock", just in ca this happens!

Light levels will be adjus within each composition u the overall picture suits concerned. Make sure that colors which have been chos blend together well and that a changes are not too abrupt unnatural.

Always allow the electrician operator sufficient time to p everything properly and clea If a memory board is being us (see pages 40-41), then all t will be far less tedious and tin consuming.

During this lighting rehears the members of the product team will all have th comments to make, accord to their particular interest in t show. These must be taken in account when possible.

A lighting designer should a to achieve his or her vision of t play, but not at the expense set or costumes. The direc will have the last word if th are any difficulties about this

Hopefully, if the pre-planni stages have been thoroug exploited and comprehens discussion has already tak place, there will be no su clash of interests.

good well-organized lighting partment will be appreciated the rest of the production sonnel and the arduous ating session may well turn to be a successful mination of earlier efforts.

e technical rehearsal

e technical rehearsal brings ether, for the first time, the ors and the technical pects of the show. This will lude lighting, sound, and ene changes. (In some tances, an initial technical earsal may be held without / actors present at all.) e purpose of this rehearsal is eliminate the inevitable iculties that result when all different departments are ally brought together.

ring this rehearsal it is at last ssible to see how all the iting cues fit into the play as a iole and how they co-linate with whatever else is ng on. A particularly difficult iting sequence may have to run through several times to sure that it can be correctly idled and that the effect is actly what is required.

ould any luminaires have to moved between scenes, en this is the time to ensure it everyone knows what is quired of them and that there sufficient time available to ect such a change.

e first technical rehearsal will pose any discrepancies in the oduction. It is all too easy to erlook some small detail, herto masked by the fact that ery department has been erating fairly independently until now.

This is the time to iron out any such problem, as amicably as possible, for by now nerves and tiredness are probably beginning to take their toll.

During the technical rehearsal, lighting states can be modified by the lighting designer as necessary. Do remember that the board operator will be very busy, especially if the board is a manual one, and do not make impossible demands of his or her time and patience.

The dress rehearsal

Every production is different. The one thing they all have in common is that any dress rehearsal should always be approached as though it is an actual performance. There may indeed be several dress rehearsals prior to the actual first night, but each one should be regarded as "the real thing" so that the timing of the production and all its potential problems can be properly and accurately assessed.

It is only if this approach is taken, that the technical departments can be confident about their cues. For instance, the operator of a manual board needs to be sure that a tricky lighting sequence is actually possible in the time allowed; and it is only thus that the designer can be sure that a lighting cue is being taken at the optimum moment. It may be that adjustments will have to be made. If lighting levels are obviously wrong, try to make any changes gradually so that the acting company are not suddenly startled by a flood of light or unexpectedly plunged into darkness.

The timing of a particular sequence may have altered dramatically due to some extra "business" the actors have introduced, or because of an awkward scene or costume change. Many minor problems arise that have not been considered before, and after this rehearsal the director may be justified in asking for a particular sequence to be re-run in order to make any adjustments and ensure that the scene will run smoothly.

Throughout, the lighting designer must take this last opportunity to study the effects of the lighting from as many different parts of the theater as possible, until he or she is convinced that every member of the audience will see just what was intended. This is particularly important with theater in the round (arena).

At last the final dress rehearsal is over. The culmination of many weeks of planning and preparation await the response of the audience. The lighting designer will have studied in detail so much that is simply taken for granted by an audience when they see a well-organized production.

A smooth and enjoyable production is only possible if the lighting has been well planned and organized. With each step, from script to lighting plan, to rigging, focusing, and rehearsal, each part of the procedure lays the foundation for the next, and must be done carefully and efficiently if the whole structure is to remain stable. Good ground work is essential if the lighting is to succeed.

Color

Using color carefully

The impact of color on a stage is always one of the most important factors. The effect of lighting with color can be particularly dramatic. If it is overdone, the result may even be catastrophic!

The way in which a lighting designer interprets color can "make or break" every aspect of a show's design concept. All the visual elements of the production can be affected by a single wash of color.

No matter what has been achieved with set or costume colors, the lighting designer can alter the end result. Sometimes, for certain scenes, it may in fact, need to be changed but in general, great care must be taken not to use lighting color effects indiscriminately.

Under normal circumstances, the color of illumination should enhance both the set and the costumes, and not fight against them. Add to this the need to use color to create atmosphere, mood, and the time of day or year; or to give the appearance that the scene is lit by, perhaps, candles or firelight — and it can be seen that this is one of the most demanding and exciting areas of stage lighting.

*Ring Round the Moon
at the Bristol Old Vic*

Color theory

Color effects for different types of shows will usually call for quite different techniques. The lighting for a variety show or a musical, for instance, would not use color in the same way as it would be used in a box set for an Alan Ayckbourn comedy.

The first two shows might well make lavish use of color, with many changes, whereas a straight play would use more subdued, natural color, of which the audience would scarcely be conscious.

Here we can deal only with the main principles of color. The final selection of what to use depends on the type of production and is very much a matter of personal choice for the lighting designer at the time.

Primary colors

A lighting designer has, as tools for the work ahead, three colors from which all other colors in light are made. These are the primaries of red, blue, and green. Together, they make white light; they are derived from white light; and various mixtures of them will create all other known colors.

Color mixing

To demonstrate what color mixing can achieve, set up a simple experiment. Take three profile spotlights of the same type and focus them to create three, overlapping hard-edged beams, as shown on the right.

So now there are three circles of white light. Add one primary color filter to each of the lights, and where all three overlap a fairly good white light is formed.

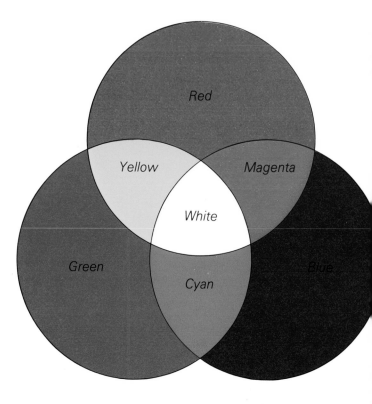

The other overlapping effects are as follows:

Green over red = yellow
Green over blue = cyan
Blue over red = magenta

Quite simply, the eye has three color receptors, — one for each of the primary colors just discussed — red, green, and blue. So any form of these colors, in any combination, can be seen by the eye. If it were possible for a color to exist without the properties of red, green, and blue, the eye would simply not see it.

It follows that if mixing the three primaries gives white light, then splitting white light should produce every different col from the red (long wav through green (medium wav to blue (short wave).

Indeed it was Newton who fi demonstrated this by splitti white light through a prism. 1704 Newton wrote, "Eve body reflects the rays of its ov color more copiously than t rest, and from their excess a predominance in the reflect light, has its color". So eve object actually reflects ma wavelengths of light.

The longer the wavelength, t redder the object; the shor the wavelength, the bluer t object, while green objec reflect the medium wavelong

hy, therefore, do we not have rig with three lights focused o the same area, and each ht fitted with a different imary color gel? Theoretically, mixing these primaries and ering the proportions of each y using different light levels), e should then be able to hieve any color required.

fortunately, in practice this ethod does not work very ell. There are several reasons.

ost importantly, the primary ls available are close — but t true — primaries. The blue is deeper color than the others d lets less light through it, so ere is an imbalance of light tput. Also, as the level of the ht is dimmed, the lamp will nd to glow towards yellow, pecially at very low level.

us the end result is a very off-hite light source being ojected through a colored ter which is not a true primary.

cause of these various perfections, an exact color production will not be hieved. Only true primary production at every level will oduce a perfect "spectrum" lor reproduction.

owever, if the shades of color quired are not too critical, the ree-color primary mixing does ork to a certain extent.

s quite feasible to use a three-lor batten which contains ch primary in order to produce teresting colors on a white oth or cyclorama. It is also ossible to use all the three imaries together to make an ceptable white.

Lighting the acting area

It is generally true that when lighting an acting area, rather lighter and more subtle tints are used to color skin tones — not the heavy colors produced by a simple primary mix, such as the one just described.

Strong coloring of the stage is best left to the back light as this will not affect an actor's face. Use this lighting structure, and then the general appearance of the stage can be made to look bright blue without the actors having to sport bright-blue faces as well!

The choice of tint or color used obviously depends on the type of illumination required — day, night, interior, exterior, or whatever the play demands.

To give some indication of the degree of color to use in normal frontlight conditions, here are a few examples which have been selected from the Lee range of colors:

Notice that "No color" or "Open white" can be categorized as a warm color. This is particularly true when used at low light levels. The range of color from a "white" light at level one to white light at full is quite astonishing.

All of these colors are most useful as "tints". They make excellent skin-tone colors because they do not color the skin so unnaturally as to make the actor look like a witch or a demon. Yet, at the same time, they will add to the general feel or mood of the scene.

Warms	Cinemoid		Lee	
Straws	73	Straws	159	No color straw
	3	Straw tint	103	Straw
Yellows/ ambers	50	Pale yellow	212	LCT yellow
	47	Apricot	147	Apricot
Pinks	51	Gold tint	151	Gold tint
	62	Pale gold	152	Pale gold
	53	Pale salmon	153	Pale salmon
	54	Pale rose	154	Pale rose
	7A	Light rose	107	Light rose
	9	Light salmon	109	Light salmon
No color		Open white		
Cools				
Blues	17	Steel tint	117	Steel blue
	40	Pale blue	144	No color blue
	45	Daylight blue	201-3	Tungstun to daylight
	61	Slate blue	161	Slate blue
	67	Steel blue		No substitute
	69	Ariel blue		No substitute

Color practice

Color correction

If white light is desired by the designer, it may seem an easy operation — simply do not put any color in the lamp. However, if the designer then uses that light at a low level, anything but white light will be produced. Instead, the stage will be filled with a yellowish murk.

Fortunately, there are gels on the market whose main purpose in life is to "color correct". Such gels can be found in the Lee Colour range. There are four gels, in various grades of blue, all of which can remove the creaminess of low-level white light.

They are:

Lee 218	$\frac{1}{8}$ C.T. Blue
Lee 203	$\frac{1}{4}$ C.T. Blue
Lee 202	$\frac{1}{2}$ C.T. Blue
Lee 201	Full C.T. Blue

These colors are also useful to create natural daylight. Normal daylight is not yellow (as one may imagine a light source from the sun to be); neither is it white. Try to create daylight on a stage with white light, and, no matter how bright this artificial light, if a shaft of natural daylight were able to come through a window directly on to the stage, then, by comparison, the stage lighting would look very creamy in color.

Add one of the above gels (the choice depends on the level of light required), and a color far closer to natural daylight can be reproduced.

The choice of color for a designer is endless. Apart from the enormous range of colors to be found in the manufacturers' color books, all these different shades can, of course, be mixed. This can be done by putting two colors in one luminaire. For more interest, a composite color can be made.

Making a composite color

A composite color is created by cutting different pieces of gel (or color filter) to fit one color frame. This can be used to great effect with a gobo, perhaps, for instance, to simulate autumn leaves. It is important that the main crossover of color should be in the center of the color frame, as this is where the beams of light emitted from t lens are most concentrate When they are finally arrange the colors can be fixed togeth with cellophane tape.

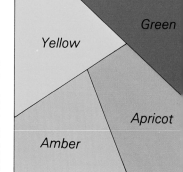

Incorrect composite

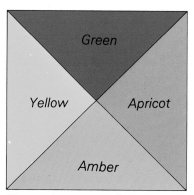

Four-color composite

Four-color composite

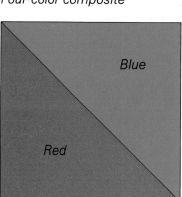

Two-color composite

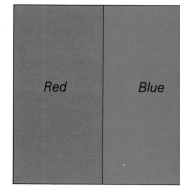

Two-color composite

pending on the type of color
ed, sometimes one of the
ors in the composition may
rink or wrinkle with the heat.
hen this happens, it usually
stroys the whole frame of
or. This may be avoided if a
ce of clear gel (called a
crificial gel) is placed behind
e frame of composite color
d in front of the lens. This gel
l help to absorb some of the
at and thus reduce the
inkling effect.

A lighting color wheel

This wheel shows some of the
colors that might be used for
stage lighting. These are all
fairly intense colors and, if used
for lighting an acting area, the
hues would be far less
saturated. (This means they
would be closer to white.)

Warm and cool colors are
shown on opposite halves of
the wheel but there is the added
complication that the yellowish-
green and lavender shades
could be defined under either
category, depending upon the
color against which they are
contrasted.

Filters may be made of dyed
gelatine, plastic,or polyester, or
colored glass. Cinemoid is a
cellulose acetate, which is very
useful as it is self-extinguishing
and therefore it does not
constitute a fire risk.

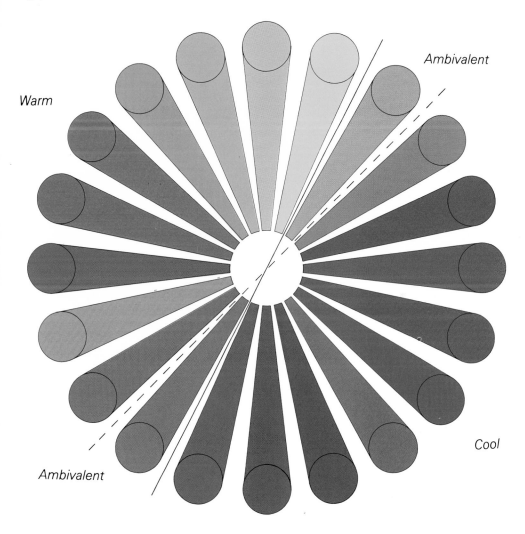

Warm

Ambivalent

Ambivalent

Cool

Choosing color

It is very difficult to give advice on what color to use for given circumstances. So much will depend on set and costume color, the director's ideas, conditions in the theater, and on the particular requirements of each show. However, here are a few basic guidelines which may be of help.

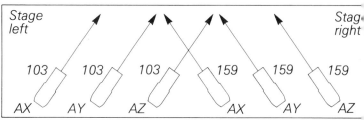
Using different tints avoids "blanket" color

The use of tints has already been discussed . When dealing with these, it will add to the general molding quality of the light if a different tint is used on each side. For instance, if a straw-tint front light is definitely required, it will look less like a flat blanket color if Lee 103 (straw) is used on one side and Lee 159 (straw tint) on the other

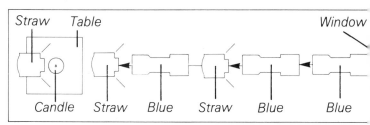
Using different colors adds realism to a light source

This can, of course, be taken a stage further when a designer is working from obvious light sources. Imagine, for instance, a room with a candlelight source on stage right, and an open window with moonlight on stage left. Two totally different colors may be used in the side light, perhaps a straw from stage right to left, and a blue from stage left to right.

The use of color in this way should greatly enhance all the sculpturing qualities of the scene, and also gives a sense of direction to the illumination.

It is important that the lighting designer does not "mush" the visual appearance of a scene. This will happen if the overall wash of color combines too closely with the set, so that it all looks rather bland and boring, like a thick soup.

For example, if a set designer chooses a bamboo color for the set, the costume designer may then follow this theme through and select a range of beige-colored costumes. The lighting designer could well think that, in order to enhance all these straw-type colors, the scene should also be lit in straw. This would be heading down the road to disaster.

Such a combination would take on a "mushy" feel, with actors and set combining and thus becoming difficult to look at.

Instead, a crisp, sharp back-light color should be used to separate the actors from the set. A front light of, perhaps, just plain white, used with this combination of colors, could look surprisingly warm and would certainly help to define the actors.

Only experience, practice, and experimenting with different gels can make a lighting designer more confident when choosing color.

Perhaps the best advice is "play safe" when first lighting plays. Generally, it is better do the following:

Light with tints from the fro and leave any heavier colors the back or side light.

When lighting with the sar color from both sides, u different shades of that color add interest.

Beware of using a blanket cc wash which is the same tone the set and costumes.

Color is a marvellous tool for lighting designer — if it is us with care. Try to be aware of effects of light and color around you.

Simply because color can ha a sensational or very drama impact, so is it also true th even quite small subtle chang in it can alter the atmosphere both in the real world, and the stage.

Color in action

ng Round the Moon

e rig consisted of a two-color
ash from the front, with 52
ale gold) and 54 (pale rose)
ing used for pink skin toning,
d Lee 201 (full CT) and 61
ate blue) for blue toning.
also incorporated a blue
cklight wash 63 (sky blue), as
ell as a very pale yellow (Lee
2 LCT).

e design called for the stage
or surrounding the set to be
lored in deep blue for the
ght scenes, and also the
tors needed to be illuminated
light emanating from a house
f stage left. For this purpose, a
om of low cross light was
iced behind each side flat on
age left. Chromoid 98 (bastard
iber) was used in the cross
ht, which lit the actors seen
age left but not the floor. This
as lit by the blue back light.

white cyclorama was used
d this was lit by Chromoid 93
front of 1 kilowatt tungsten-
logen floodlights. On some
casions a string of Chinese
iterns had to appear to
iminate the stage. In order to
nforce this effect, the area
side the set was covered by a
ash of break-up gobos with
rying composite colors.

pling

e rig construction of *Kipling*
as designed in such a way
at the man, Kipling, (who was
rtrayed by Alec McCowen)
uld be highlighted effectively
followed wherever he moved
the stage.

is was achieved by normal
ea separation (described on
ges 76–81) and each area

Ring Round the Moon

Kipling

was lit in the following manner:
The front light consisted of Lee
203 ($\frac{1}{4}$ CT) and open white. A
sepia toning was required and
this was obtained by "toppy"
side light (that is side light which
is moving slightly towards
overhead lighting), colored in
Lee 205 ($\frac{1}{2}$ CT orange) and Lee
204 (full CT orange).

The rear projector seen in the
photograph provided constantly
changing effects, but also often
reverted to the original slide's
image of a window. For this
purpose a backlight wash of Lee

202 ($\frac{1}{2}$ CT) was used to imitate
daylight from behind.

The photograph actually shows
the "preset", which had its own
set of "specials"; a down or
toplight wash of zenith blue
(gelatran 60), and a "special"
focused on each of the furniture
pieces. The luminaires were set
just down stage of the "180
degree relationship" to each
piece, so as to strike the front of
the articles. Lee 203 was used
in each "special" to diminish the
creaminess of the white light at
low level.

Color in action

When the Wind Blows

Because of the restricted area separation plan, the coloring of each area varied a great deal. The living room had a two-color frontlight wash of Lee 162 (bastard amber) and Lee 201 (full GT). The kitchen had a front wash of 73 (half straw) and 45 (daylight blue). There was a sidelight wash of 54 (pale rose) in the living room to mimic light-bounce from the rosy walls; a side light of 3 (straw) in the kitchen (where the walls were yellow) served the same purpose in this area.

The outside area was lit, in the main, with Lee tungsten-to-daylight filters (201-3 and 218). This gave clarity at all levels with the 201 producing a good graying color at low level to add to the effect after the bomb had been dropped.

Peter Pan

The nursery scene pictured here was lit and colored in a fairly natural way to save the "magic" for later in the show. A warm and cool frontlight wash was used; pink (52 pale gold) and blues (45 daylight blue and 40 pale blue).

As most of the scenes were at night, a very "toppy" side light was used for highlighting each area in a composite color of 32 (medium blue) and 63 (sky blue). The side lighting consisted of a three-color wash, using amber, pink, and blue respectively. These were numbers 2 (light amber), 78 (salmon pink) and gelatran 60 (zenith blue). A backlight wash of gelatran 64 (medium blue) completed the main-rig construction.

When the Wind Blows

Peter Pan

The picture shows the use of a warm front light in pale gold, cooled just slightly by the blue front light to improve its clarity. The medium-blue back light produced blue halos when room lights were switched off, so as to imitate the moonlight through the windows. Extra pink toning from the side (to simulate the night lights abo the bed), was provided by kilowatt Fresnels colored in L 157 (pink) and set on ea downstage perch. This p highlighting can be seen in white sheeting. The co structuring in this picture sho perhaps the least complica coloring used in the show.

... e Bengal Lancer

... e set of *The Bengal Lancer*, ... ich was designed by Bob ... owley, consisted of twenty-... e tons of sand, a large ... nount of gauze, and a few set ... ces. This simple but very ... ective approach to the set ... t a good deal of scope for the ... hting designer.

... e photograph here was taken ... The Studio at the Haymarket ... eatre in Leicester, where ... rly limited lighting resources ... plied. Its subsequent transfer ... The Lyric in London enabled ... e production to erect a rather ... ore elaborate rig, while still ... aining the same color format.

The sand, which was reddish in color, was lit by top light in Lee 238 This added extra "heat" to the appearance of the play, which, for the most part, was set in India. The gauzes were lit in blues and pale mauves and contrasted well with the rear cyclorama, which was lit in salmon colors (as shown in the photograph).

The transfer to the Lyric allowed the opportunity to reverse these colors and use salmon gauzes and a blue or mauve cyclorama, as well as the original colors. This provided for greater variation and heightened the effect of different localities within the show.

The set pieces were lit as individual sections in side, top, and front light, and the varying colors were used to create variety in the show because, although the set did not change, the localities, the time of day, and the seasons of the year, did alter considerably.

There was just one cover of front light in warm tints (not shown here). Lee 103 was used from one side, and Lee 162 from the other. Any cooling of colors was achieved by the pale-blue side light, which was colored in Lee 203 and Lee 202 ($\frac{1}{4}$ and $\frac{1}{2}$ CT).

... e Bengal Lancer

Color in action

The Gondoliers

Opera can be one of the most exciting forms of theater for a lighting designer. It usually offers scope for a wide choice of color and light angles within lavish sets. This is one time when the lighting designer will probably need to pay as much attention to lighting the set as to the acting area.

The set shown here from *The Gondoliers (Act Two)*, has eleven flown pieces, each of which was separately lit. The colors used were two-fold, one selection to enhance the color of the set, and the other to exaggerate these chosen colors. For instance, to enhance the color of amber on the borders, Chromoid 98 (pale golden amber) was used, but to exaggerate it yet further, Chromoid 134 (golden amber) was also used. The coloring on the walls was designed using the same principle, graduating to the color of the floor.

There were several dance numbers in the show and when these were taking place, a full awareness of the set was unnecessary. The photo here shows the dancers isolated within the set, which is just visible behind. The color used here included a blue Chromoid 93 for back light, which gave a deep overall color to the stage. A low cross light of L117 (steel blue) from stage right and Cinemoid 69 (ariel blue) from stage left gave the dancers extra form. As the lights were focused straight across the stage and shuttered from the floor, the deep-blue back light, which illuminated the stage floor, was not affected. A wash

1 The Gondoliers

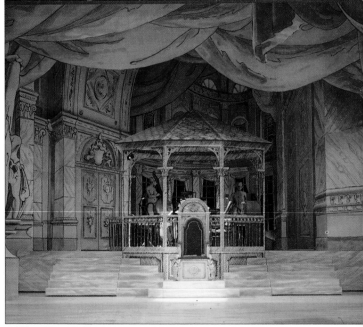

2 Dancers isolated within the set

Lee 162 was used at low level from the front to enhance all the in tones.

can be seen in this otograph, the set for Act One esented a lighting problem; le light could not be used from stage, except from a wnstage perch position.

e scene here, showing the tors "in song", was left in a rly "normal" lighting state. cause of the pastel-colored costumes, great care had to be taken not to destroy their delicate shades by using lighting which was too heavy.

Light tints were used to front light in warm and cool, using Lee 162 and Cinemoid 45 (daylight blue). Side light from the perches was in a very light blue to add further clarity (as can be seen in the highlighting of the actors downstage left). The border of painted washing was lit with Lee 218 ($\frac{1}{2}$ C.T.) which simply color-corrected the white light, allowing the natural color of the painted washing to show through. The floor coloring was created by the back light, thus ensuring that the actors' faces and costume fronts were not affected. Although the back light was fairly heavy and used deep blues (Chromoid 93), primary reds (Chromoid 106), and deep orange (Chromoid 158), a fairly neutral back light was achieved by mixing them.

Actors in song

Special effects

Put quite simply, special effects are fun! Whatever aspect of production may be concerned, whether set design, properties, makeup, or the lighting, any departure from the routine or humdrum is always welcome; as such, special effects can be particularly exciting and very rewarding for all involved. They provide a good opportunity to be inventive and to use one's imagination to the full!

There are, of course, bound to be a few problems and frustrations, as with any other area of lighting, but perhaps the greatest difficulty of all is knowing when to stop! It is always a temptation to overdo a special effect, particularly if it has been rather difficult or expensive to contrive. There may be a grim determination to use it to the full, to the detriment of the overall end result.

None the less, when producing and using special effects, the lighting designer has a unique opportunity to be creative and ingenious. Do experiment with different methods, both old and new, and explore all the various techniques and pieces of equipment that are available to you. If conventional methods will not produce exactly what is required, then a new special effect may have to be invented. The scope is enormous.

Many special effects are described in this chapter. These include the moon and stars, rain, lightning, and swirl clouds; rippling water, f effects and neon signs. So are produced by techn means, such as projecti gobos, and ripple machin Others need only very sim equipment, such as light bo: or a gauze screen, while stunning galaxy of st requires only foil and bl, cotton thread.

Not all the special effe discussed in this chapter strictly "lighting". They h, nevertheless been includ because it is usually the light department, with all technical know-how, that asked to stretch its limits produce the very wide variet effects that may be needed

Stars

Making stars

Stars can be created in number of ways, and which method is best to use really depends on the design and restrictions of the set concerned.

Projecting stars

Stars can be projected. This can be done by using a star slide in a projector, or by fitting a star gobo into a profile luminaire.

Using a star cloth

Stars can be "wired" into a cloth. The stars are, in fact, made up of pea bulbs, or any pin-point light source. A small hole is pierced in the cloth and the bulb is then poked through. It can be successfully wired from the back. This method is obviously very time-consuming, but has the advantage of being both very effective and easily controllable. If the wiring of so many bulbs is too daunting a prospect, use instead a ready-made string of clear or white Christmas-tree bulbs.

Hanging stars

Hanging stars are made of balls of foil, attached to black cotton thread, and flown to the required height.

To create a "galaxy", simply tie a number of lengths of black cotton thread to the house bar at irregular intervals.

Now tear off pieces of foil and roll them up into $\frac{1}{4}$ inch (6mm) balls. They can then be attached to the lengths of black cotton thread by twisting them around the threads, being careful to avoid too regular a pattern.

When this is complete, the cotton thread can then be swagged to form a "galaxy".

By side, top, or up lighting the arrangement, the foil will be illuminated so as to twinkle effectively. The black cotton thread will be scarcely visible.

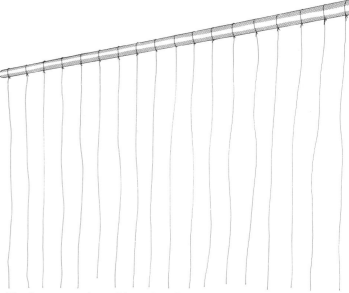

Black cotton thread hanging from house bar

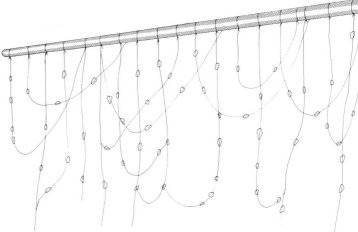

Using cotton thread with foil to make a galaxy

The moon

Projecting a moon

The most common method of creating a moon is to project it. If a full moon is required, a profile should be "irised" to give the correct size and then focused on the cyclorama or cloth. An acceptable full moon may be produced this way; a crescent moon can be created by using a gobo in the luminaire. It is important to remember when projecting a moon, that the light source should really be at right angles to the material on to which it will be projected. Otherwise a full moon ends up looking rather egg-shaped! This right angle is sometimes difficult to contrive from the front. Back projection may alleviate this problem, as the light unit remains unseen and can therefore be lowered to a suitable position without being compromised by having to hide behind part of the set.

Obviously if the cyclorama or cloth is inclined at an angle (as in *The Recruiting Officer,* discussed on pages 166-71), then the position of light must follow suit in order to maintain the correct angle.

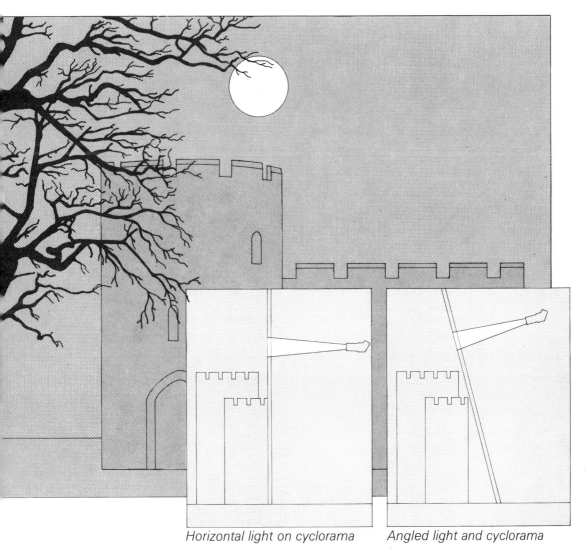

Horizontal light on cyclorama   Angled light and cyclorama

Using a light box

Another method of creating a moon is by using a "light box".

This is simply what its name suggests — a source of light contained within a box. It is usually made of wood with the front removed, and fitted with lamps, which are wired into the box unit.

The type of lamp used will largely depend on the depth of the box and the brightness required. If a shallow box is used, strip-lights will be the best option as then the whole light fitting will be suitably narrow. If a deeper box is chosen, domestic light bulbs can be inserted. Pearlized bulbs will help diffuse the light. Even so, there may be some hot spots. This can be alleviated if silver-top (or reflector-top) bulbs are used instead.

The front of the light box can be covered to suit the design requirements. Often the front is made of calico which will help to disperse the light over the whole area. If the light box is being used to create a moon, then a piece of black card or wood can be cut to the required shape, depending on how full the moon is meant to be. This is then fitted to the front of the light box.

A light box of this type (now made into a moon box) is usually hung directly behind a cyclorama or backcloth. It is important that the box is positioned so that it is virtually touching the cloth or it will not create a sharp enough image.

This is probably the best method of creating a moon, as any shape can be quite easily produced, and there are distortion problems. Of cour the light box can be used many other different effe Any shape can be cut, or frett out of a wooden sheet and t fitted to the front of a light b

Neon signs

Light boxes are often used make an effective illumina sign when the set requires o Color gels can be fit between the box and its fr cover to color the sign and mimic the effect of neon frosted gel will help dispe hot spots.

Colored light bulbs can also used to color the image on front of the box. If there are t or three separate circuits bulbs in the box, and each cir is fitted with different colo bulbs,(perhaps red, yellow, a blue), these can be made flash in order, so that the s continually changes color.

A sun box

If the lighting box is to be us as a sun box (as opposed t moon box), then the co could be made to fade fr whitish yellow to golden am as the sun sets. The effect be greatly enhanced supporting the sun box on flying line and then slo lowering it down the back of cyclorama, so the sun "sets

If the particular color of b required cannot be rea purchased, then it is possible paint an ordinary pearled bul to dip it in FEV (French enar varnish). Many different co and tints are available.

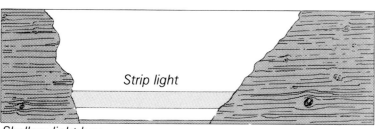

Strip light

Shallow light box

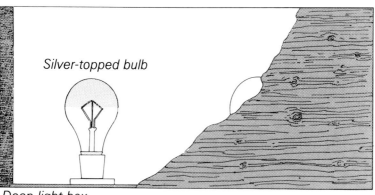

Silver-topped bulb

Deep light box

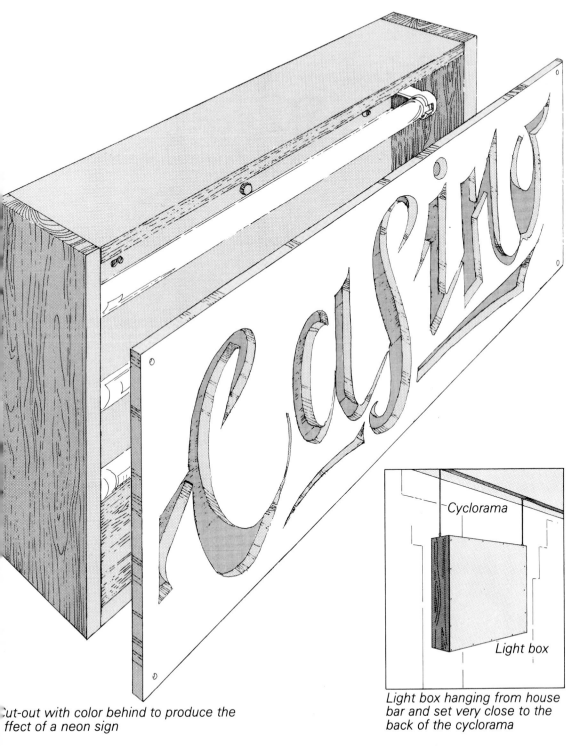

Cut-out with color behind to produce the
effect of a neon sign

Light box hanging from house
bar and set very close to the
back of the cyclorama

Cyclorama

Light box

Clouds

If possible, try to utilize two different projectors, both fitted with a cloud effect, and then focus them on to the same area. Make sure that one effect is running at a slightly faster speed than the other. The clouds will then move across each other and this will result in a more realistic effect.

If the projection is to be directed on to a cyclorama or a sky-cloth, then it is a good idea to obtain a gauze (scrim) and then set this just down stage of the cloth. By projecting on to the gauze, an image will be created on both the gauze and the cyclorama, as the light passes through the mesh of the gauze. This creates a wonderful 3-D effect.

Clouds across a moon

Unfortunately, if a moon effect has been used (as described earlier on pages 115-6), then simply projecting clouds across this will not give a true representation of how clouds move past the moon. This is because when clouds cross the moon they become silhouettes.

The only way to achieve th effect is by using two projecto with cloud effects. The fir projector has a "positive mas to project the moon and th clouds that go across it. Th second projector will have "negative mask" to project th clouds surrounding the moon

The masks can be made fro card or lithoplate. It will soon k discovered that the negativ shape may be difficult suspend in the center of th effect aperture. It may therefo be best to paint the maskir required on to clear aceta which can be far more easi taped into position.

Even when using an identic cloud disc for each effect, th cloud images will be unlikely completely coincide. It impossible to fully co-ordina the way they enter, cross, ar leave the moon. This really doe not matter, however, for would take a very keen eye spot exactly what is happenin

The effect may be furth enhanced if the project producing the moon is set a higher intensity than i negative counterpart. The linir up of the two projectors critical; the positive ar negative moons must overla each other exactly.

Static clouds

Meshed gobos can be used form very good clouds, if r movement is required. This is, fact, the cheapest methc of creating projected cloud because quite ordinary profi luminaires can be used, ar there will be no need to hire special projector.

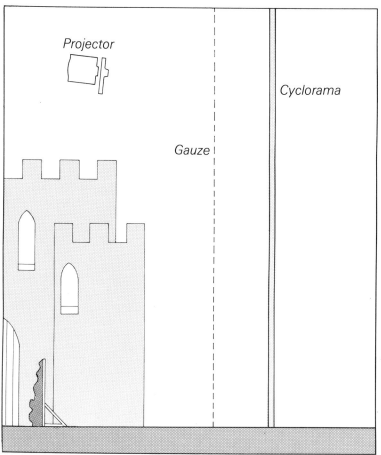

Using a gauze (scrim) and cyclorama creates a 3-D effect

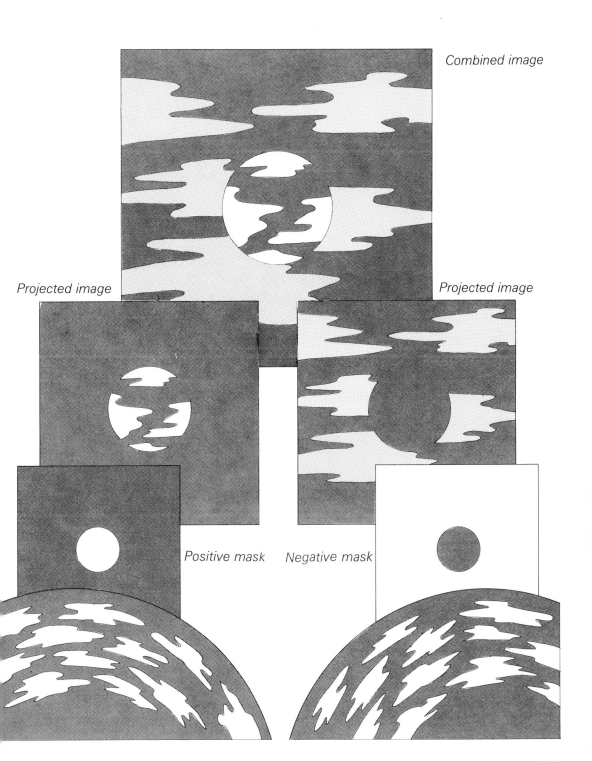

Combined image

Projected image

Projected image

Positive mask

Negative mask

119

Snow, water, and lightning

Snow

The most realistic snow effect is achieved by using a snow bag. The bag is set in the flies and from this overhead position, it releases hundreds of paper dots which float gently to the stage floor.

This method, however, is not always acceptable, because of the inevitable mess it causes! An alternative is to use a projected-snow effect, but this, unfortunately, often ends up looking rather ridiculous, largely because of its repetitive nature.

To some extent, this problem can be overcome by using two projectors focused on to the same area. If possible, try to obtain two snow-effect discs and make sure their dot formats are different.

A snow effect is achieved by using a glass disc which has been painted black, except for a pattern of clear dots. Light can pass through these little spaces and the pattern formed will look remarkably like snowflakes.

If the snow effects in the two projectors are run at different speeds, the illusion of falling snow will be rather more convincing. In this respect the effect is similar to a moving-cloud projection.

Water

There are several water effects available. These include running water, rain, waves, and ripples. The first two are usually created by using discs in the same way as for clouds or snow, but waves and ripples are effected rather differently.

A moving-water effect is created by fluted glass pieces. Instead of rotating as discs do, these glass pieces move up and down within the effects unit. The result is rather like gentle waves furrowing the surface of the sea.

Ripples can be made by using a ripple machine (or projector). This ripple machine consists of a rotating metal tube into which ripple patterns have been cut. A light source is fixed behind it and the two units are mounted in a metal case.

Forked lightning

If forked lightning has to ▮ projected on to a cyclorama over a set, then the mo convenient method is to use forked-lightning gobo set whi is inserted into a profi spotlight. Some manufacture (or rental companies) m convert a profile luminaire incorporate a strobe bulb. Th in turn, must be plugged into strobe unit. The high-intensi flash given by the strobe bu greatly enhances the forke lightning effect.

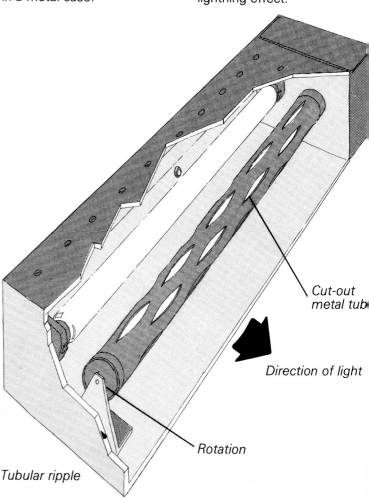

Cut-out metal tub

Direction of light

Rotation

Tubular ripple

trobes, light curtains, and auze transformations

obes

boscopic lights work on a
tive-discharge" principle.
bes can be used very
cessfully to simulate any
hing-light effect, and they
particularly dramatic when
ating film on an antiquated
ector or when used to make
ors appear to be performing
 old-fashioned silent movie.

ord of warning, however, is
ded here. Strobes must be
d only with extreme caution
 only for very short periods
me. There are, in fact, legal
uirements regarding this and
se should be checked. Apart
 the unpleasant effect on
 eyes and the sense of
ince, they may induce an
eptic fit. Some insertion in
 program to give prior
ning of their use is essential
nd then keep well within the
kimum time allowed.

ht curtains

ght curtain is, as the name
gests, simply a curtain of
t. Lighting designers in the
p-music" industry have used
t curtains for many years.
y have a very powerful
 dramatic effect, especially
en a number are used, one
ind another in lots of
erent colors.

it curtains may be usefully
ployed in theater lighting. (A
cription of how a light
ain was used in *When the
d Blows* is included on
es 175-6.) A light curtain is
duced by a row of Par lamps
ctly next to each other. They
 be separate Par cans (see
e 32) or combined units
ch make a batten of Par

Elevation of a light curtain

lights. These battens of Pars
may be of the low-voltage type.
Whichever sort they are, the
object is that each unit must
give an intense, near-parallel
beam of light.

The batten or row of Pars is set
at an angle, pointing towards
the audience (so this is, in
effect, back lighting). The
steeper the angle, the better the
result will be.

The intense light the Pars
provide will illuminate any dust
or dirt particles floating in the
atmosphere, as they are
"caught" in the beam. The more
dense the dust or dirt, the better
the effect. Wafting smoke
through the atmosphere will
make it "dirtier" and it will then
be virtually impossible to see
through the light beams. Thus,
apart from the visual impact a
light curtain creates, it can also
be put to a practical use. It will
effectively mask whatever lies
up stage of it, so a scene change
can therefore be hidden behind
a light curtain, or an actor might
"appear from nowhere" through
the veil of light.

Gauze transformations

Used skilfully, a gauze (or scrim)
transformation can really create
magical effects. Through what
appears at first to be a solid
scenic cloth, a whole scene can
materialize quite unexpectedly.
However, the lighting of a
scenic gauze must be done very
carefully to achieve the "magic"
successfully.

Whether or not the gauze is
painted, the steeper the angle
of light which illuminates it, the
better the result. If the gauze
does not incorporate a painted
design, then back lighting can
be considered. The main
objective is to prevent too much
light passing through the mesh
of the gauze and illuminating
whatever is up stage of it.
Lighting the gauze in this way
will make it appear solid.

Any actors, magical scenes, or
new sets that are to be lit and
seen through the gauze must,
of course, always be lit by
luminaires that have been set
up stage of the gauze. It is
essential to remember this
when planning the rig.

Very careful timing will be
needed as the lights are brought
up on the scene behind and
simultaneously reduced on the
gauze in front so that the
change-over can take place
perfectly smoothly. The stage
will then appear to be suddenly
and mysteriously transformed,
as if a solid medium has melted
away and a new scene has
been conjured from nowhere.

The effect is really so simple to
perform and yet it can lend quite
a stunning or beautiful element
to a scene.

Gobos (patterns)

Gobos (or cookies) are not used solely for special effects, but are often an integral part of the main rig. Sometimes they may be used so subtly that the audience are quite unaware of their presence. On the other hand, their impact may be so striking that they become an effect in themselves.

As explained earlier (on page 29), a gobo is a metal plate with whatever shape is required cut or etched out of it. The size of the plate will depend upon the luminaire for which the gobo is intended. The determining factor is the gate size of the luminaire, as this is where the gobo (or an iris or mask) will be fitted. The shape that has been cut in the metal plate can then be successfully fitted and projected in a profile luminaire. Some other types of luminaire are unsuitable as the gobo must be inserted between the light source and the focusing lens.

Projecting images and texturing

Gobos are most commonly used to project the images of windows, tree branches, or leaves; or to create "break-up" patterns on the stage.

Break-up refers to a method of texturing which can be very useful when lighting a set or stage floor. A piece of scenery, or perhaps a wall or house front, may look rather bland if it is simply washed with plain light. This is particularly so if the surface is flat. Lighting the surface with break-up gobos and using an appropriate soft focus will add texture and interest. This can be further enhanced by the use of a composite color (see page 104). A simple break-up gobo will consist of just a metal plate which has been drilled with a series of random holes. Leaf gobos, intended primarily to create woodland effects, can also be used for very simple texturing, provided that the luminaire is suitably defocused.

Almost any shape can projected with a gobo. Ma shapes are readily availal from gobo manufacturers a come complete with th respective holders. Thr examples are shown below.

If the required shape is r available, manufacturers v usually etch them to order.

Realistic leaves

Skyline

Medieval

king a gobo

os can be quite expensive,
it may be worthwhile
mpting to make a simple
o yourself. All that is
uired is some thin metal,
ferably aluminum-based, so
it will be easy to cut.
ters' lithoplate is ideal. If this
ot available, then the base
oil plates or trays (perhaps
n the local "take-away"
aurant) will suffice.

t cut from the lithoplate or
tray a piece of metal that will
the gate size of the
inaire — it is advisable to
e the piece a few inches
r than the gate size so it can
asily fitted and removed.

t cut out the particular
pe required. If it is to be used
break-up gobo, then simply
or punch holes all over the
e. If, on the other hand, a
cific shape is needed, then
should be cut out with a
sharp knife or a Stanley
le. Begin at the center of the
al piece and be careful not
ut too near the edges or
e of the shape may be lost
ng the focusing.

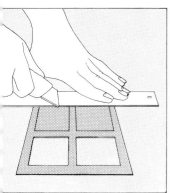

ting out a window shape
a modeling knife

Composite gobos

Gobos can be used to create a composite effect to make, for example, a projected stained-glass window. These can be achieved most effectively by using a special composite gobo set, made specifically for this purpose. This set usually consists of four or five gobos, each of which will create one piece of stained-glass window.

Each of these gobos must be fitted to a separate luminaire, but every one of these luminaires must be of exactly the same type. The images projected from these luminaires are then focused one on top of another, until a complete stained-glass window effect is formed. By putting a different color filter into each luminaire, a very realistic and attractive effect can be achieved.

Green

Yellow

Blue

Red

White

Complete window

Gobos

Creating moving images with gobos

Surprisingly, gobos can also be used to make a moving image. The method is similar to that used for composite effects. To create, for example, a water fountain, four gobos would be used. The first of these will be cut into a fountain shape, and the other three will have been pierced with water droplet shapes. The droplets should be cut out in slightly different places on each of these three gobos, so that their respective positions fall progressively lower on each gobo.

Once again four luminaires are required, and each will be fitted with one of the gobos. Focus each projected image so that it overlays the others. Every luminaire must have its own circuit. Then the lights can be made to chase each other. By quickly flashing each luminaire in turn, the water appears to move. The light in the luminaire which contains the basic fountain structure, will, of course, remain constant.

Using mesh in gobos

The use of fine mesh in the manufacture of gobos is now becoming very popular. mesh will allow shapes to suspended in the middle another design, and realistic clouds can also made by using this method

A word of warning is ag necessary here. Gobos fitted to one of the hottest pa of a profile spotlight. The cer of a gobo will very quickly h up and glow red hot. Extre care must be taken when fit or removing them. If luminaire involved has been even if for only a very short tir always use gloves or a cloth handle the gobo or its holde

A mesh-tone cloud gobo

Projection

ere are a number of very good ecial effects that can be ojected. These are readily ailable and can be very useful. cenic projection has not been cluded in this discussion but e notes regarding angle tortion at the end of this ction will apply to most forms projection.)

lighting designer may be led upon to create "moving" ects as well as static ones. ten some movement will be eded to add to the natural pearance of clouds, snow, iter, smoke, and fire.

most cases, a call to a local eater rental firm will secure a table projector and effects it. In principle, the mechanics e the same for all the various es of projector and effect. All u will need to know is the ittage of light required from e projector, the throw (the tance from projection to age), and the image size. It is m the throw and image data it the objective lens size is culated. Provided the type of ojector and the "gate" size is own, it will be possible to rk out the lens size.

a guide, if the projector is ing a 3 inch x 3 inch (75mm x mm) gate, then the lens size n be calculated by using the art on the right.

us, there are three units ich make up the total effect. ese are the projector (or light urce), the effect, and the jective lens.

e effect must be fitted to the nt of the projector, and the is must then be fitted to the nt of the effect.

Most moving effects are simply produced by using a painted glass disc which rotates by means of a motor inside the effects unit. The painting will represent the image which is to be projected, such as clouds, running water, fire, smoke, or falling snow.

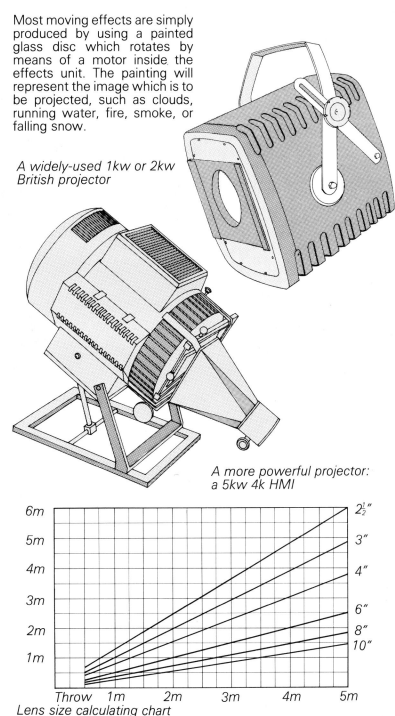

A widely-used 1kw or 2kw British projector

A more powerful projector: a 5kw 4k HMI

Lens size calculating chart

Lens size calculating chart

◇Pyrotechnics

It must be pointed out that maroons, flash powder, and transformation powder are all potentially dangerous and if used or stored incorrectly, then an explosion or fire could result. Always be sure to follow these instructions in order to maintain safety standards.

1 In the UK, a licence is required before explosives can be kept or stored. Check with your local fire or police department and follow any advice given.

2 It is advisable to contact the fire or police department, in any event, to see whether you can actually use pyrotechnics (The building where the production is to take place may be deemed unsuitable for such a potentially dangerous exercise.)

3 Always store the pyrotechnics in a metal container when they are not in use, and preferably in a room that has been set aside and labeled "Explosives Store"; so that no-one can be in any doubt as to the nature of the contents therein.

4 **Never** smoke when using, wiring, or loading flash boxes; or when handling transformation powder or flash powder.

5 **Always** unplug the flash box or device you are working on.

6 Mark clearly all plugs and switches that will be operating any explosive device and then make sure everyone concerned is warned about them.

7 Follow the manufacturers' instructions to the full.

Maroons

Maroons are used to create the noise of explosions by actually exploding. They come in three basic sizes which contain varying amounts of an explosive material encased in cardboard. They are somewhat similar in construction to a "banger" type firework. They are electrically detonated by using a special pyrotechnics detonator, and easily fired from an ordinary small six-volt battery.

Bomb tank

Maroons must always be placed in a suitable, metal open-ended container such as a dustbin or galvanized water tank, to contain the explosion. The open part of the "bomb tank" can be covered with chicken wire to prevent any large pieces of maroon leaving the tank, but never put the maroon into a completely closed container or it may well be turned into a potentially dangerous bomb!

If more than one explosion required during a show, the more than one maroon can be placed in the bomb tank, and wired back to a separate switch. Sometimes, however, one maroon may destroy another when detonated. This can be prevented by placing the maroons as far apart from each other as possible.

Do make sure that everyone involved in the production whose activities might take them in the vicinity of the bomb tank, knows exactly where it and when the maroons are going to be detonated; then hopefully, the area can be kept clear at the appropriate time.

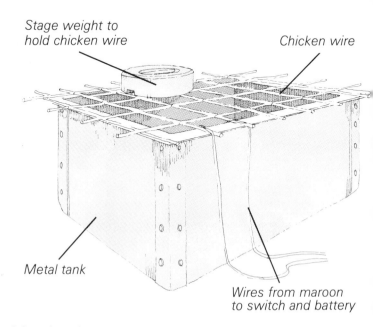

Stage weight to hold chicken wire

Chicken wire

Metal tank

Wires from maroon to switch and battery

A bomb tank

...sh powder

...sh powder is a very fast-
...rning powder which is used
...create flashes. It is highly
...ammable and great care
...st be taken when it is
...ndled, so it is important to
...ep it well away from any open
...me or strong heat sources.

...sh box

...lash box is used to contain
...flash powder prior to and
...ing the detonation and is
...de of metal. As the flash
...wder is usually ignited by
...mote control (usually from
...newhere off-stage) the flash
...x contains two electrical
...minals (live and neutral).

...he old days, the system was
...ly primitive. The terminals
...uld have been shorted out
...h a small piece of fuse wire,
...d a level teaspoon of flash
powder was piled over the fuse
wire. When the flash was
required, the flash box was
plugged into a mains supply, the
fuse wire melted, and the flash
powder was ignited. It was
rather a case of keeping fingers
crossed that the right wire
melted and the building
survived the experiment!

Nowadays one can hire or buy a
flash-box system that is rather
more sophisticated and reliable.
It uses a premade flash
cartridge that simply plugs into
the flash box. It is detonated
from a low-voltage power
supply, situated in the switch
box containing the "fire" button.

Pyrotechnic fuse or detonators

Pyrotechnic fuses can be used
to detonate flash powder but
their explosive force is very
directional so the flash powder
must be placed in just the right
position. However, by using
cigarette papers, it is quite a
simple matter to make a home-
made flash cartridge.

First, roll the cigarette paper
around a pencil and then stick
the glued edges together as
normal. Put the pyro-fuse in one
end of the paper cylinder, with
the wires outermost, and then
twist the paper around the
wires to hold the paper on to the
detonator. Pour flash powder in
at the other end of the cylinder
until it is almost full. Finish
making the cartridge by twisting
the paper together to hold the
flash powder safely inside. The
home-made cartridge can then
be placed in a metal box and
wired to a switch and battery.

Premade cartridge systems and
pyro-fuses can turn out to be
very expensive if a great many
flashes are required. It may be
considerably cheaper to use
resistors as detonators and a
car battery as a power supply. If
$\frac{1}{4}$ watt 10 ohm carbon resistors
are used, then the car battery
should have no trouble in
"blowing" the resistor.

Transformation powder

Transformation powder is a
slow-burning powder which
can produce a colored flame.
Several colors are available and
some, such as green and
amber, can be very effective.

Transformation powder must
not be mixed with the fast-
burning flash powder because
the force of the latter may send
out a shower of the powder
when it is still burning. It should
therefore be held in a metal
container and lit by a taper.

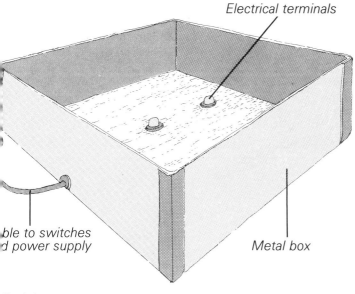

Electrical terminals

...ble to switches
...d power supply

Metal box

...flash box

Dry ice and smoke

Dry ice

Dry ice is frozen carbon dioxide. Gloves must be worn when handling dry ice as it sticks to the skin and burns. Also, when breaking up blocks, cover the ice with a sack or cloth to prevent splinters flying about and injuring someone's eyes.

When dry ice is melted in boiling water, the resulting vapor is heavier than air and will therefore hang near the ground. Special containers called dry-ice machines are available for sale or hire. These incorporate an electric element to boil water and consist, in effect, of a sealed box with one small opening from which the vapour escapes. A "cage" is included to hold the dry ice and, to some extent, the effect can be regulated by lowering or raising the cage in and out of the boiling water. These machines are designed to provide large amounts of vapor, but they can be expensive to buy. A small bath tub which is filled about half full of hot water and set on a trolley will provide the same effect. Never overfill the tub as the action of dry ice melting is extremely violent.

To assist the production of vapor, it is a good idea to break up the dry ice into small pieces. The greater the surface area available to the hot water, the better the reaction. Wrap the dry ice in a cloth or sack to avoid any pieces flying around, and then hit it with a hammer.

Storage

Storing dry ice can cause problems. If you put it in a domestic freezer, any food will be ruined and the dry ice will still deteriorate. The best method of storage is to seal the dry ice in an airtight plastic bag and then embed this in a box full of expanded polystyrene. This may keep the dry ice stable for a day or two. Really, the only way to ensure that there is always enough dry ice available for a performance is to collect it from the supplier a few hours before each night's show.

Smoke

Smoke can be created in a number of ways. The safest method is to use a smoke gun. Glycerine oil is forced through a heated pipe by either a CO_2 gas bottle or by an integral air-pressure pump. This smoke gun will produce vaporized glycerine oil which looks and acts very much like smoke. However, it does smell rather sweet and, unfortunately, it will also cover everything in a fine layer of glycerine oil.

Another smoke gun which available can be easily refil by simply screwing on a "sp can". These refills can selected from a small range different types of smoke eff Each effect will look differ according to how long smoke stays in the air bef finally dispersing. For exam one type will produce "steaming kettle" effect, wh the smoke disperses alm instantly; while anot provides a lingering effect, suggest, say, a misty morni Thus, smoke guns are ideal many effects, either to prov copious amounts of smoke swirl gently over the stage perhaps to "seed" the air so li beams are seen more clearl

Smaller amounts of smoke be made by heating a "s burning" smoke powder o heating element. This is nc safe method and, moreover, fumes produced may be rat strong smelling!

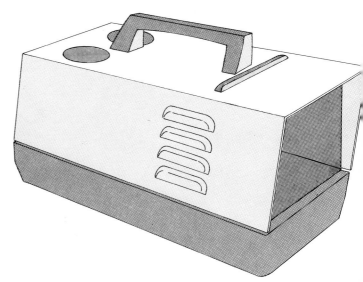

Portable smoke box

lickering fires

effective fire can be created
making a wooden grate and
n using flickering colored
t bulbs set behind it to give
impression of a glowing fire.
using fluorescent starters
ich can be bought as spares
fluorescent light fittings) and
ing them in series with light
bs, the bulbs can be made to
ker on and off indefinitely.
e speed at which the bulb
kers can be altered by

changing either the wattage
size of the bulb or the starter.
Use three or four different
colored bulbs (to include red,
yellow, and amber), with one on
constantly and the others made
to flicker; in this way an
excellent copy of a real glowing
fire will be created.

Fluorescent starters have only
two connections and it does not
matter which one is connected
to the supply or bulb.

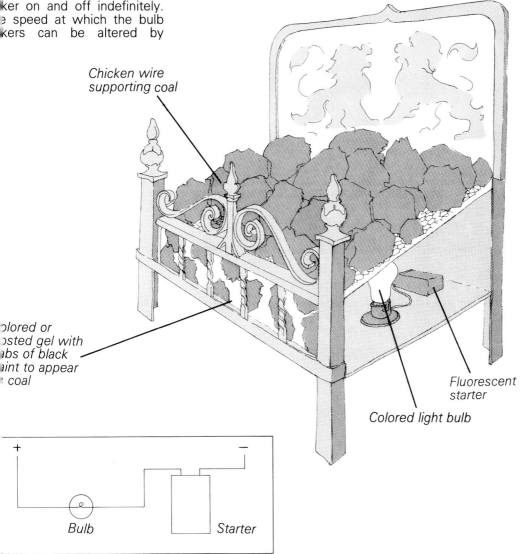

Chicken wire
supporting coal

plored or
osted gel with
bs of black
aint to appear
coal

Fluorescent
starter

Colored light bulb

Bulb   Starter

cuit diagram for wiring starter to light bulb

Oil lamps

Electrically operated oil lamps

When a practical oil lamp is required on stage, the obvious way to control it is to use a mains-powered bulb fed via a dimmer, allowing the level of light output and the fading up or down to be controlled with the rest of the lighting rig. If, however, the oil lamp has to be carried around the stage by an actor during the show, it will then have to be battery operated. It is possible for the actor to fade the lamp up or down via a small potentiometer inserted in the oil lamp battery circuit. However, if the lamp has to work independently, then radio control is the answer.

Mains operated oil lamp

Use a pair of wire cutters to remove the wick and the mechanism for lowering and raising it, and then enough room can be made to fit a mains operated lamp holder. A gallery containing a lamp holder can also be bought to replace the wick gallery.

Battery operated oil lamp

Removing the wick and mechanism (as for the mains operated lamp) provides ample room for a small lamp holder such as an MES (Miniature Edison Screw). This can be securely fixed with either nuts and bolts or by binding it in with stiff wire. If this is done carefully, the space created by the removal of the controls to lower and raise the wick, should be sufficient to allow a potentiometer to be inserted. A wirewound potentiometer will be required for this.

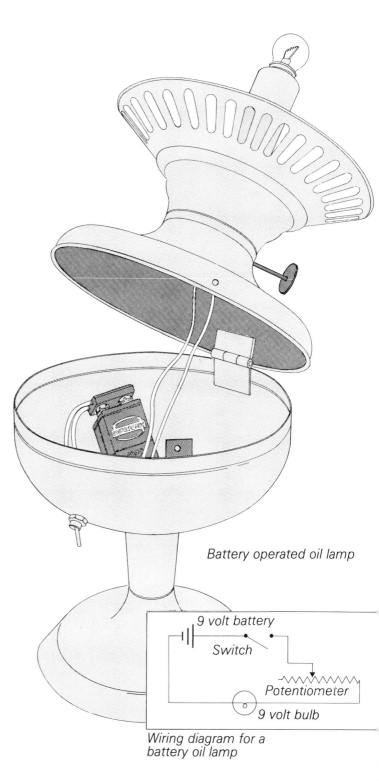

Battery operated oil lamp

Wiring diagram for a battery oil lamp

he only problem left is where to hide the batteries. The most obvious place is in the container that carries the oil, just below the gallery. It is quite likely that the opening that is left when the gallery is unscrewed is too small for the batteries to fit in, so the oil lamp will have to be modified to accept them. Using a hacksaw, cut very carefully round the container, just below the lip. Take care not to bend or scratch the lamp.

Now use a small brass hinge and carefully solder it to both pieces of the lamp, so that both parts will hinge open and close. Nuts and bolts with spacers could be used instead. These will prevent the lamp from, being bent out of shape when the flat hinge is fixed to the round lamp. At the opposite side of the lamp, fix a small piece of metal to the lid and drill a hole through this and through the bottom part of the lamp to make a catch to hold the two hinged parts together. The oil lamp can be opened to enable the batteries to be placed in the newly created, large opening compartment. A switch should then be inserted in the circuit to isolate the bulb from the battery and conserve energy.

Radio controlled oil lamp

Radio control equipment (as used in model kits) can be made to fade an oil lamp up and down. A transmitter, receiver, and DC motor speed controller are all that are needed. The DC motor-speed controller doubles as an excellent dimmer. Both receiver and speed controller can be hidden along with the batteries in the oil container. The aerial however should be kept outside

to avoid any loss of signal. It can be hidden, for instance, in the glass shade or funnel. The system can be used to run the standard torch bulb, as for the battery operated oil lamp. All the manufacturers' instructions should be followed in order to connect up the radio control equipment correctly. Make sure there is no interference.

Candles

Candles can be made very simply by using half (or one and a half) inch diameter, white plastic tubing, as found in a domestic water system. Simply fix a bulb in at one end with the wires feeding it running down the inside of the tube to a battery. If a candle tray is being used, this will effectively hide the switch and battery. A strip of tracing paper placed around the bulb and twisted into a flame shape, will make this candle look more realistic.

There are several electrical candles made for the theatre. One type can be bought in battery or mains form. It uses a specially shaped bulb which looks like a candle flame and is held in the candle on a tiny gimbel-like arrangement. This allows the bulb to move gently about as if the "flame" is wavering in the wind.

The other type uses the same PVC tubing as the home-made candle but it has an electronic circuit embedded in it. This produces a flicker between two bulbs built into the "flame" part of the candle. The effect created may appear a little wild, but it does resemble a candle in a strong wind. This candle can be run only from a 9v battery.

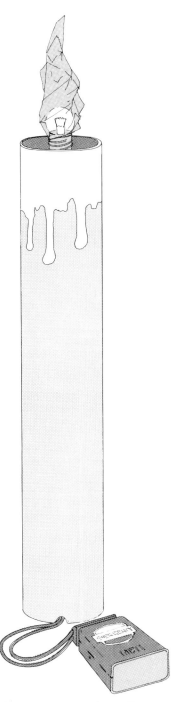

A battery operated candle

131

Notes on projection

On choosing a projector, find out the focal lengths and angles of the various lenses that can be used with the lamp: for instance, a 4 inch lens could give a 10 foot square image at 12 feet and an 8 inch lens a 6 foot square picture at 20 feet. Do a scale drawing on tracing paper of these angles

Superimpose this tracing on to the ground plan to find out which lens is most suitable and to check how far away the projector needs to be from the screens (or, if the projector can be in only one place: how far away the screens need to be from the projector)

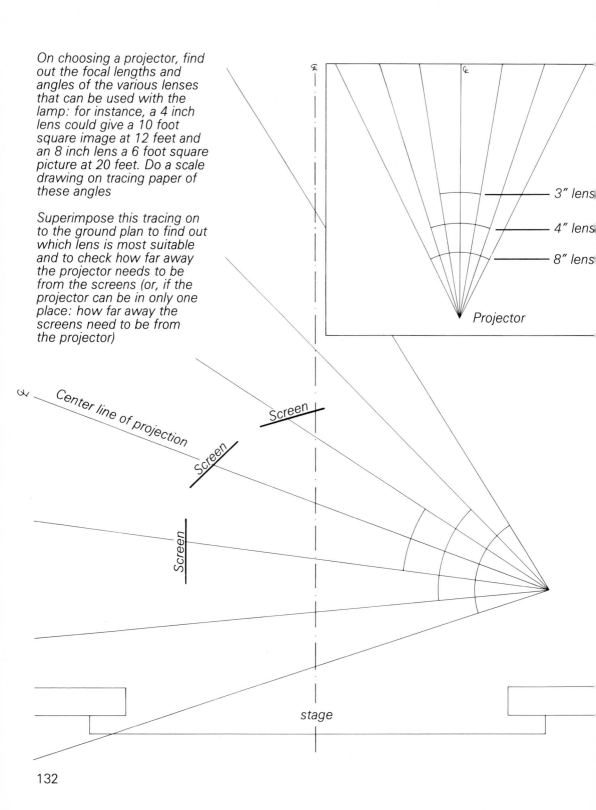

3" lens

4" lens

8" lens

Projector

Center line of projection

Screen

Screen

Screen

stage

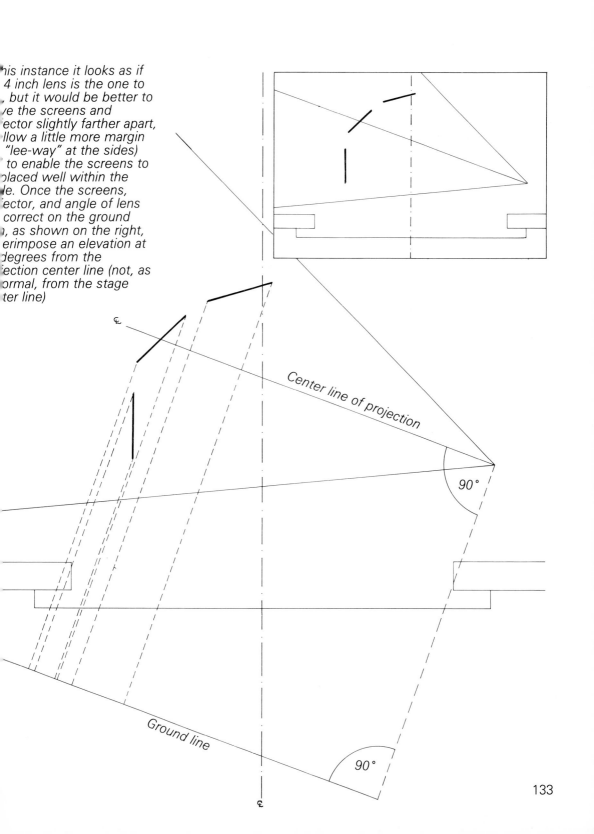

his instance it looks as if
4 inch lens is the one to
, but it would be better to
e the screens and
ector slightly farther apart,
llow a little more margin
"lee-way" at the sides)
to enable the screens to
placed well within the
le. Once the screens,
ector, and angle of lens
correct on the ground
, as shown on the right,
erimpose an elevation at
degrees from the
ection center line (not, as
ormal, from the stage
ter line)

Center line of projection

90°

Ground line

90°

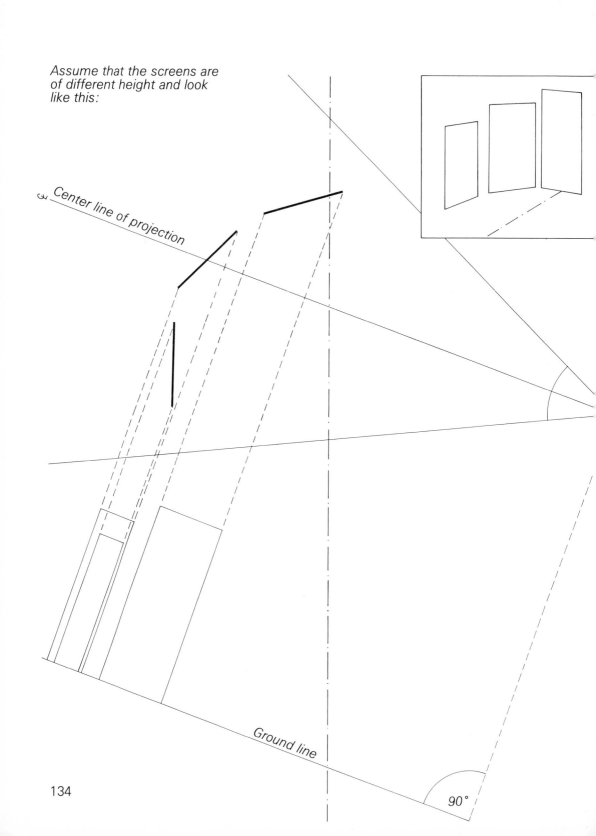

Assume that the screens are
of different height and look
like this:

Center line of projection

Ground line

90°

ish superimposing the
evation to scale. Now, find
e height of the projector.
s is decided by several
tors. For instance, the
her the luminaire, the

nearer the actors can be to
the screens without casting
shadows on them. However,
the placing is usually
determined by purely physical
factors, such as the heights of

bars, or which rostra are
actually available for the
standing or hanging of
projectors. When this is
determined, center the
screens again in the lens
angle, using the same
tracing paper as before

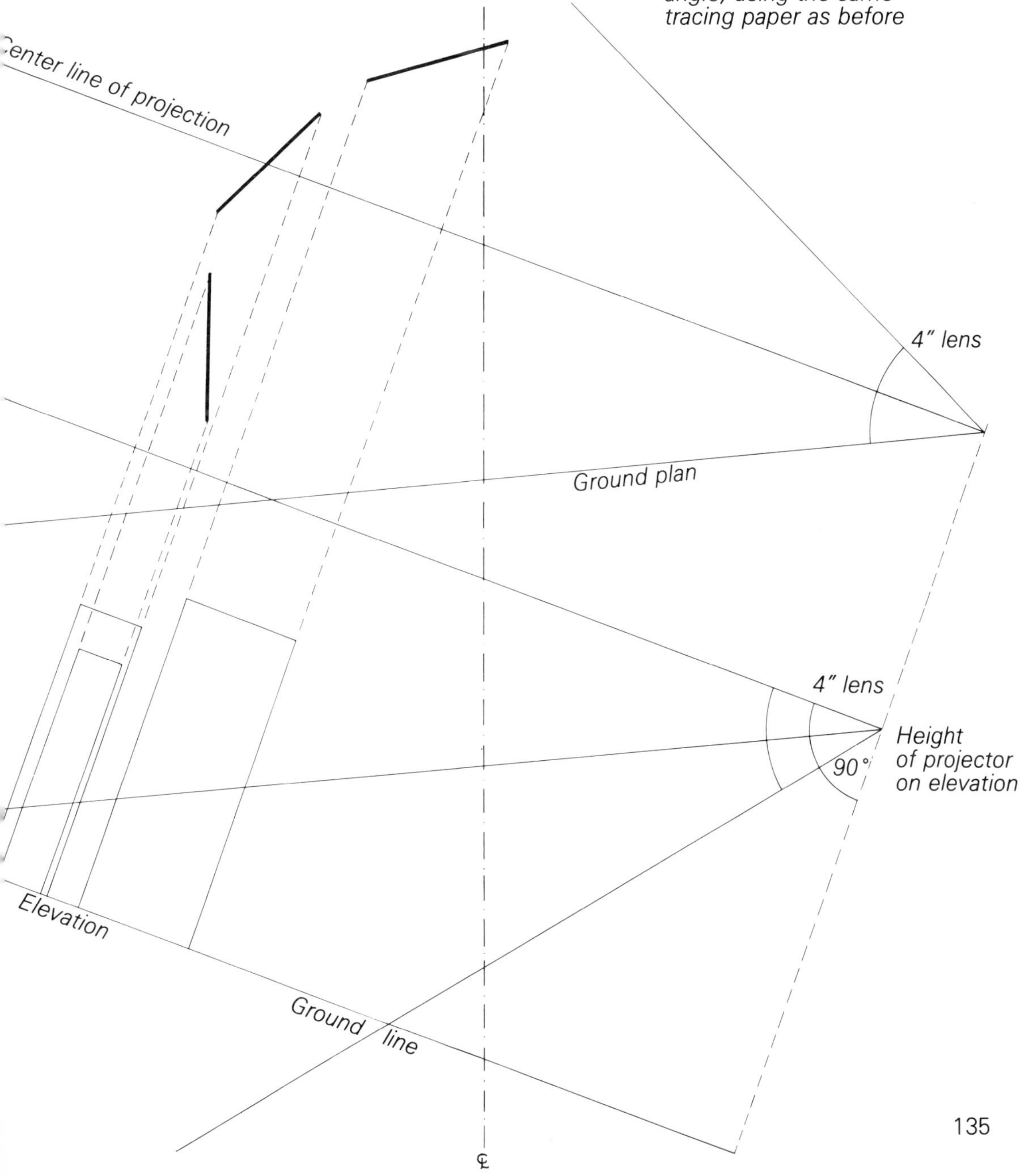

Center line of projection

4" lens

Ground plan

4" lens

Height
of projector
on elevation

90°

Elevation

Ground line

Take the actual dimensions of the slide cartridge of the projector concerned, that is, the dimensions of the particular slide that will project the image. (This varies with the type of projector.) Draw its elevation at 90 degrees to the center line of the elevati projection, at the point wher its dimensions coincide with the outside limits of the projection angle

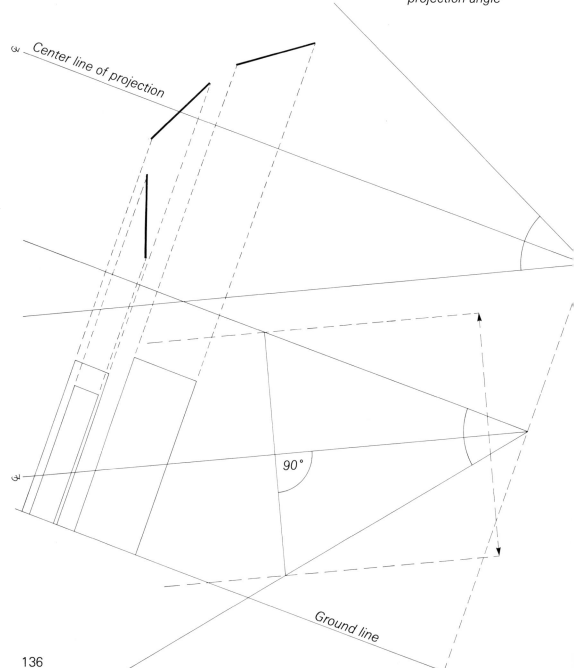

Center line of projection

90°

Ground line

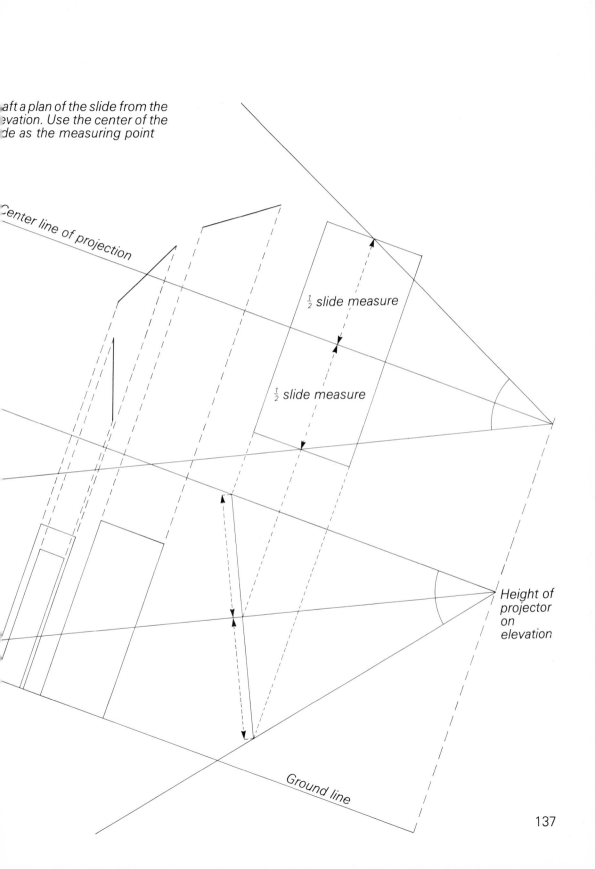

...aft a plan of the slide from the
...evation. Use the center of the
...de as the measuring point

Center line of projection

½ slide measure

½ slide measure

Height of
projector
on
elevation

Ground line

137

At this point, the drawings are ready to use. Now it will be possible to start working out exactly how to make the slide

Draft lines from all corners of the screens through to the projection point on both plan and elevation. It is helpful to

letter and number the corne so as to keep track of what happening. The diagram shows the necessary markir

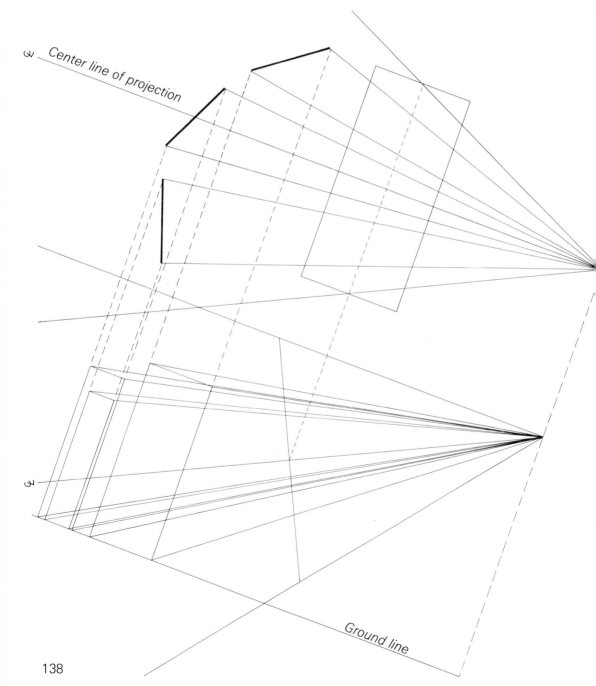

Center line of projection

Ground line

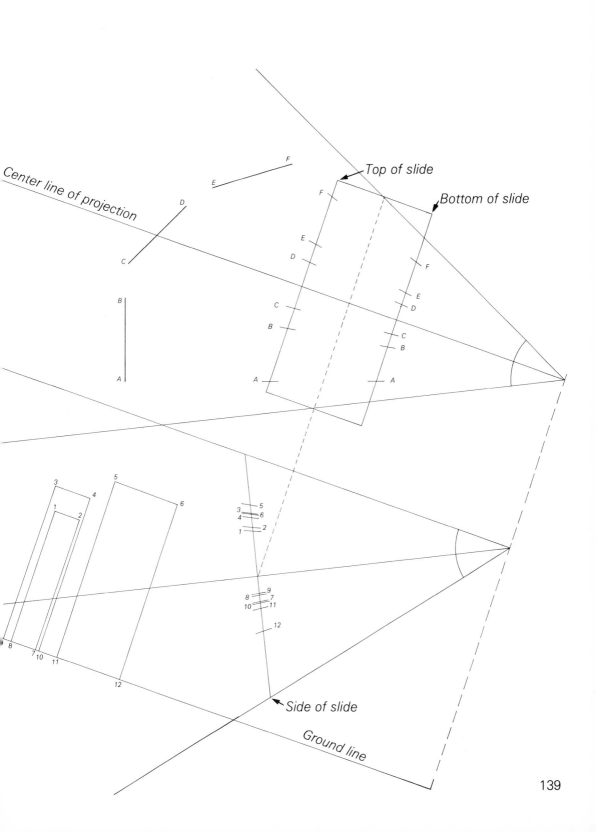

Center line of projection

Top of slide

Bottom of slide

Side of slide

Ground line

139

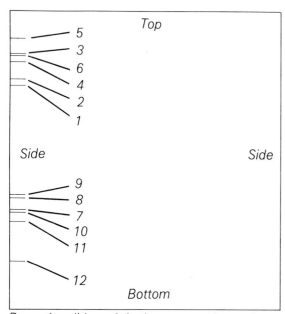

Draw the slide so it is the correct size and enter up the elevation marks on the side

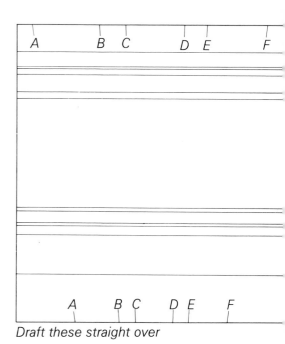

Draft these straight over

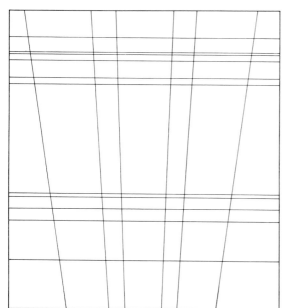

Add the marks from the top and bottom of plan to top and bottom of slide itself and then draft through

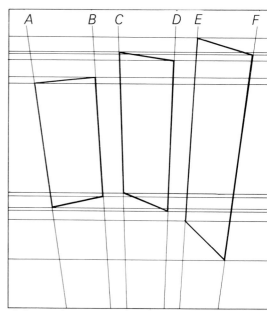

Join up the appropriate co-ordinates to form the image of the three screens on the slide, as shown above

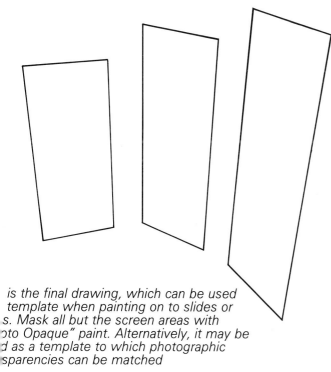

... is the final drawing, which can be used
... template when painting on to slides or
...s. Mask all but the screen areas with
...oto Opaque" paint. Alternatively, it may be
...d as a template to which photographic
...sparencies can be matched

Notes on the use of photographic slides

A wide-angle lens is normally used for projection. Ordinary camera lenses are most unlikely to have a lens of equal width, so the photographer will be unable to place the camera in the exact position on the model that the projector would occupy. Therefore the camera must be moved farther back, to bring the screens into range. Try to match the template with an "enlarger" afterwards. Less distortion occurs if the camera is moved away fom the model horizontally, at the height of the projector, and is kept parallel with the center line of the plan. This method is better than attempting to raise the camera along the center line of the elevation

Lighting the stage with limited resources

The earlier section in this book on *Lighting the stage* (pages 62-89) dealt mainly with how to light the stage in ideal conditions with a free choice of equipment. More often than not, however, the lighting designer of a small or amateur company may have to be rather more adaptable. The venue is quite likely to have limited resources and a lighting budget that is virtually non-existent. Not only may there be a limited number of luminaires available, but also on the amount of power and the quantity of dimmers that can be used.

Do not despair! There are a number of ways that these restrictions can be overcome or minimized. Very often it is simply a case of using "lateral thinking", looking at the stage concerned with a completely open mind and not necessarily expecting to be able to employ all the conventional equipment in the conventional way. Perhaps a glance through the historical survey (see pages 10-19) might be a very useful undertaking. Earlier lighting experts coped remarkably well without any of our modern engineering and it might be possible to make use of some of their ideas; at the very least, it will serve as a reminder that the situation should never be regarded as impossible.

The particular problems of how to provide both warm and cool washes, sufficient acting-area cover, as well as any color a highlighting required, with wl may seem to be inadequ equipment, will be discuss This chapter explains how use differing light levels, versalility of luminaires, cro plugging, color wheels, a home-made lamps. Admitted many more specific difficult may well need to be overcor but still the same principles v apply. Exploit whatever available. Use imagination a initiative. Do experiment v new ideas; and old ones! compromized only by the saf of the undertaking. Rememl the prime objective is to light1 actor. Follow these guidelir and the limited resources m well become stepping stones greater creativity.

Control and color

Control boards

The most difficult problems to deal with are those presented by a primitive control board. If, for instance, the theater has only a two-scene preset board or, at worst, a single-scene preset board with no group facilities, then the lighting for the show must be designed with this restriction in mind. The director should also be made aware of this limitation very early on because any fast and complicated lighting changes are made virtually impossible, and this must be borne in mind during production and planning.

There are, however, many aspects of limited equipment that, with a little imagination and resourcefulness, can be dealt with and accomodated into the overall scheme.

Providing a warm and cool wash

The lighting designer will generally aim to incorporate a two-color wash. In other words, every luminaire used for front lighting should have a counterpart alongside focused into exactly the same area; this second lamp will be fitted with a different color so that the stage can be given a warm or a cool color wash.

Although this is the ideal situation to achieve, it can prove quite a strain on the available equipment. If a one-color wash only can be used, this will immediately halve the amount of luminaires that will be necessary. It is perfectly acceptable to do this, especially for a one-state show. A day-lit box set could be quite

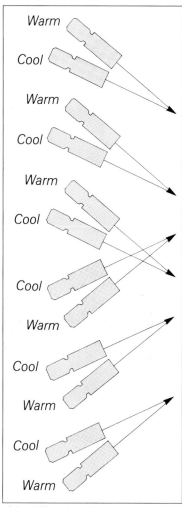

Ideal illumination

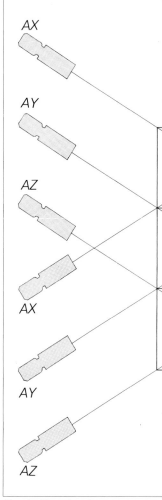

Basic illumination

adequately covered by a one-color frontlight wash.

The problems occur when this is not acceptable — when the stage must have both a warm and a cool atmosphere. One method of dealing with this situation is described here. First light the acting area in the normal way, but this time use only one luminaire each side to light the same area.

Use a neutral color for this ba lighting so that the whole sta can be lit quite simply, with any color tones.

Remember that a lumin. with no color is not true wh (see page 104), especially low level. It will probably nesessary, therefore, to us color-correction gel to retain neutral quality of white lig (Try Lee 203 or $\frac{1}{4}$ C.T.)

144

ving achieved this overall neutral cover, the next step is to find a way to light the stage to both warm and cool.

The desired effect can be achieved by using the front or the back lighting to provide a warm or cool wash. If the designer chooses the front lights to do this, then a wash of the whole stage (in both a warm and a cool wash) will have to be provided by just a few lamps. This is quite feasible — after all,

economy of lamps is exactly what is required in this instance.

If this is the situation, it is useful to remember that you should choose "wash" luminaires which have twice the rated power of the "area" lamps. Thus, if 500 watt area lamps are being used, then choose 1000 watt wash lamps; and if 1000 watt area lamps are being used, then choose 2000 watt wash lamps. On an average stage, it is possible to provide a wash in

this way with only two lamps; one focused stage left of center and the other focused stage right of center. They must be rigged in such a position that the spread of light from the luminaire will cover the whole stage; this may mean using a rather flat angle. Add a color wheel to these two luminaires and the designer will have a choice of five color washes. (There are five color positions on one color wheel.)

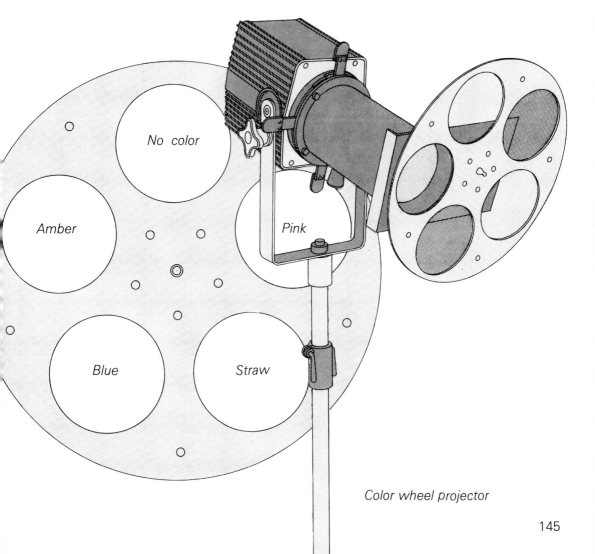

Color wheel projector

145

Using available resources

Now the designer has the advantage of the whole stage being lit in a controllable way, by use of area-cover luminaires. Moreover, the mood and the temperature of the stage can be altered by means of the colored washes. The diagram below shows a typical frontlight focus plan when using this method of lighting.

It can be quite justifiable to have the colored wash provided by the back lighting rather than the front. This can be particularly useful if any obvious light sources (which may be usefully employed to color the stage) are already coming from the top or from the rear; for example, sunlight or moonlight.

The same principles apply as before. Wash the stage with the chosen color; leave highlighting of actors' faces and special areas to area-color luminaires.

Although this second metho color washing works wel most situations, it may be t in certain circumstances, i not sufficiently adaptable.

For example, the designer n be faced with a situation wh there must be controlla areas in both a warm and a c color. Obviously, it would impossible for moonlight provide both these colors.

Color wheels

If the dimmers, as well as lamps, are a limited resour the designer might t consider using color whee One should be fitted to e lamp down one side of the and then the neutral-li method can be used on other side.

It can be seen that color whe may be "life savers", coming the rescue in a difficult situati They are certainly cheaper t hiring the equivalent in e lamps and dimmers. They c however, be a problem to se and synchronize, so designer must allow suffici time to do this properly.

A well-organized color-wh system can overcome m difficulties. On the other han it is not put together correctl can lead to hours of frustrat and be a total waste of time. do it properly or not at all!

Using relative light levels

It should be remembered t light levels are relative. instance, if there is a gen luminaire shortage, a bri daytime scene may seem problem. However, by adjust

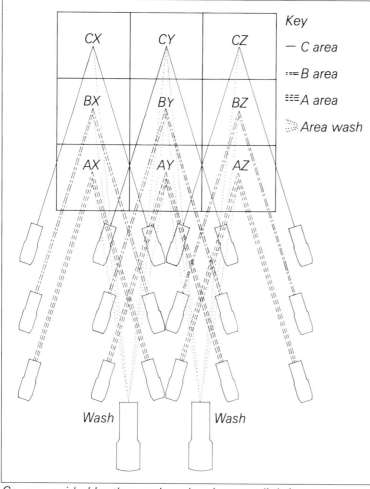

Cover provided by the wash and acting-area lighting

Key

— *C area*

=== *B area*

≡≡ *A area*

⋰ *Area wash*

CX CY CZ

BX BY BZ

AX AY AZ

Wash   Wash

eyes of the audience orehand, the illusion of ghtness can be created. e, for example, a situation ere the first scene of a play es place in full sunlight or ds simply to be seen as a y bright scene. If only a few inaires are available, ensure t, when the audience walk the house lighting is as dim s practically possible. Under circumstances should it be ght and glaring. Then, as the selights go down, try and ve the house in darkness for moment or two before ging up the lighting state on stage. Then the relative ghtness of the stage lighting have far more impact, and audience really believe they looking at a brilliantly lit ne — even though the ount of kilowatts lighting the ge may be quite small.

e bright setting is not in the ening scene but instead ows another scene in the y, then try to avoid high light els in this preceding scene. If tive light levels are used sibly, then differentials are ays possible, even with all lighting rigs. Sometimes, neaters which do not impose type of restriction, a sudden y bright lighting state may be

too much of a shock to the audience's eyes. If this is the case, the lighting state should be brought up, initially, to only 80 per cent and then slowly lifted to full light. Do this gradually, taking a minute or two to effect the change in lighting levels, and then the audience will not detect that this is happening.

"Dead" areas

A designer should always be aware of every inch of the stage which is being used. When lighting with limited resources, it is wise to be aware also of every inch that is not being used. There may well be "dead areas" where a double-cover wash would be a total waste of time; or there may be areas which are used so occasionally that they can be quite adequately lit by a special for just those few moments.

Making the most of the luminaires

Sometimes there may be only unsuitable types or amounts of equipment available. There could, for instance, be far too many profiles and not enough Fresnels; or too many Fresnels and not enough floods. When

this happens, it is often possible for some pieces of equipment to double up for others. It is always worth experimenting with different luminaires to discover their full potential.

For example, if a frosted gel (particularly the new Hamburg variety) is fitted into a profile, it will then give a fairly good soft-edged light, similar to the Fresnel. In the same way, if the lens is removed from a Fresnel, this can convert it into a very plausible floodlight. (Careful use of the barn doors can even transform this into quite a well-controlled light.)

Dimmers

The amount of luminaires may not be the only limiting resource factor for a lighting designer. A lack of dimmers may also be an impediment. With a degree of forethought, this problem can be reduced considerably by either "pairing" (or "cross-plugging") the lamps.

Pairing lamps

Although it is usually desirable to have one lamp per dimmer, it is not always necessary. Lamps lighting the same area or the same piece of set can be paired together to share the same circuit or dimmer. If floods are lighting a cyclorama, these can often be coupled together, perhaps as many as four or five to one circuit, depending on the wattage of the lamps and the loading of the dimmer. Great care should be taken, when pairing up lamps, that the dimmer rating or circuit load is not exceeded. It is also most important to make sure that the correct cable rating is used.

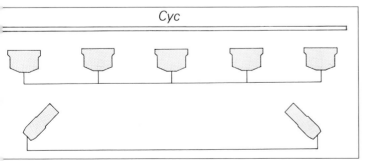

eral luminaires can share one circuit

Cross plugging

A designer will soon realize that not all the luminaires on the rig are necessarily being used in each scene. Therefore it is often possible to cross plug.

This is a system whereby several luminaires, particularly specials, may be able to share the same circuit because they use it at quite different times.

For example, if there is a play with three different acts, it is quite feasible for one circuit to control three different luminaires being used at separate times — provided that cross plugging between the acts is possible. Obviously, all these luminaires must terminate at the plug point of the dimmers and should not "pair" on the bar.

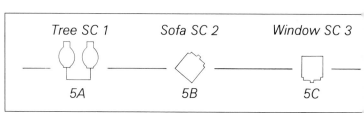

Tree SC 1	Sofa SC 2	Window SC 3
5A	5B	5C

Specials sharing the same circuit

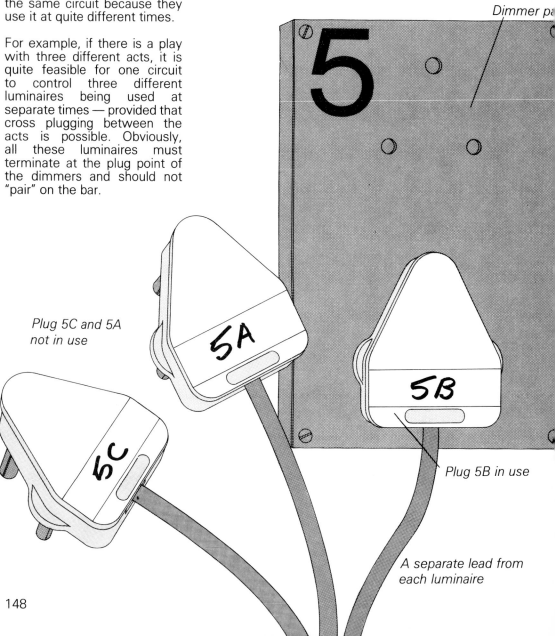

Dimmer pa

Plug 5C and 5A not in use

Plug 5B in use

A separate lead from each luminaire

Home-made luminaires

ng "home-made"
ninaires

other economy is to avoid
ng upstage luminaires where
y are not strictly necessary.
en lighting a door backing, or
de a small alcove, for
ance, it is a pity to use stage
inaires if they are in short
ply. A string or batten of
nary household bulbs will
t a door backing quite
ciently. If a slightly more
trollable light source is
ded, then it is a good idea to
unt the light bulb and holder
 biscuit tin or a clean, large
n can. It is most important to
th the metal can.

is worth noting that a
ector-type bulb will give
n more direction to these
me-made" luminaires. Color
s can, in fact, be cellophane-
ed to the front of these
keshift luminaires. Do make
e that there is adequate
tilation by drilling holes in
base of the bean can (or in
top and bottom sides of the
cuit tin). This will stop the
ing of the cans becoming
ecessarily hot.

rking within the discipline of
ted resources may well be
 "norm" for some lighting
igners. These designers,
 the fortunate ones for
om it is a rare occurrence,
 need to use their ingenuity
 experience to deal with the
iculties that arise. Hopefully,
ideas in this chapter will help
ve some of the problems. At
imes, have a regard for the
ety of any measures taken
 then fulfil all the aims of the
ting designer as best you
 — within the particular
traints imposed.

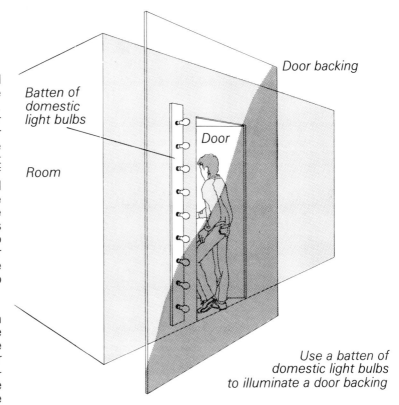

Door backing

Batten of
domestic
light bulbs

Door

Room

*Use a batten of
domestic light bulbs
to illuminate a door backing*

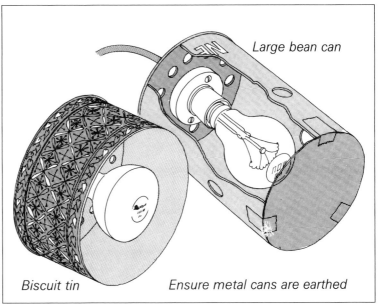

Large bean can

Biscuit tin

Ensure metal cans are earthed

*A home-made luminaire can be made from a bean can or from
a biscuit (cookie) tin*

Basic electrical theory and safety

The handling and installation of lighting equipment should never be undertaken without knowledge of the electrical principles involved. This chapter explains basic electrical theory and how to keep well within the bounds of safety. Unless the lighting mechanic is a practised electrician, professional advice will be essential. Do not ever attempt to "work in the dark" or you may end up doing just that!

Electricity consists of charged particles called electrons which exist in every kind of matter.

Electrons are pumped through conductors by a generator or battery. This generator exerts pressure, which is measured in volts, on the electrons.

An electrical circuit can be likened in many ways to a pumped water system. For instance, the greater the force a pump exerts on the water in a system, the greater the water flow (measured in gallons per minute). The greater the force exerted by a generator or a battery on the electrons, the greater the electron flow will be (measured in amps and called the current).

In a water system, changing the size of the pipework affects the water flow. A wider pipe will allow more water to flow through, in a given time, than a narrower pipe of the same length. This is because the narrow pipe resists the flow more than a wide one. Similarly, electron flow can be affected the size and type of mate that the electrons pass throu

This is called resistance an measured in ohms. Resista is defined as the ratio betw the electron pressure (volts) the electron flow (amps).

The formula for resistance
$$\text{Resistance (R)} = \frac{\text{volts (V)}}{\text{amps (I)}}$$

The symbol for resistance R (measured in ohms). symbol for electron pressur V (measured in volts), and symbol for electron flow I (measured in amps). T knowledge may be useful later calculations.

◇Electricity

Making and using electrical energy

Electrons must complete a circuit in order to flow. Every battery or generator has two terminals and if a wire is connected between these, electrons will then flow from one to the other. The terminals are labeled + (positive) and — (negative), as shown below.

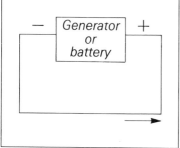

A simple circuit

Energy is given to the electrons in an electrical circuit by pumping them from a low voltage to a high voltage. Energy is released by letting electrons fall from a high voltage to a low voltage.

Whenever the electrons flow from a higher to a lower voltage (through a piece of wire, a motor, or some other electrical apparatus), their energy is transferred to the equipment. If the energy is not recovered, by using it for mechanical work for instance, it simply heats up the wire or device.

So the circuit in the diagram above will allow electrons to flow but the energy generated will be entirely wasted in a form of heat. This is caused by the resistance of the wire, rather like friction might produce heat.

By inserting a device that utilizes the electrical energy in the circuit, we can make the energy work for us.

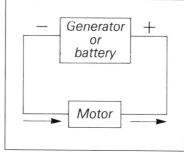

Utilizing electrical energy

Alternating current

So far we have considered current flowing in one direction only. This is called "direct current" or DC. Alternating current circuits work just like the DC type, except that the current is first travelling in one direction and then in the other. The current will literally alternate above (positive) and below (negative), zero amps, making one complete cycle.

The frequency of alternating current is measured in hertz. One hertz equals one cycle per second. Electricity supplied to industry and for domestic use consists of alternating current at a frequency of 50 hertz in the UK and 60 hertz in the USA.

How electrical energy controlled

There are only two w electrical energy can controlled. The first is simpl control the amount of ene that is put into a circuit by battery or generator. Howe this is not always possible. voltage of a mains supply, instance, is constant.

The second way is to regul the energy, using varia resistance to "throttle" electricity supply. In pract terms, this means that electr energy can be controlled only switching on and off, or regulation.

The mains electrical supply

The electricity generated power stations is normally in form of a four-wire syst (three phases and one neutr

There are three coils inside generator. One end of each is connected to a common po called the neutral. The other e of each coil remains separ and is called live. The coils spaced equally around generator at 120 degrees — t provides a "phase ang (between voltages) of 1 degrees. Because of the pha angle, the three phases,

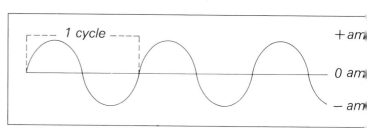

An AC waveform

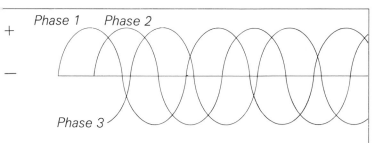

+

−

Phase 1   Phase 2

Phase 3

A three-phase AC waveform

waveforms, reach their peak voltage at different times.

The electricity produced at the power station is transformed up to a very high voltage and then distributed. At substations the voltage is transformed down to the mains (local) level. Substation transformers have three coils, which have their respective neutrals connected together. This neutral point is connected to an earth electrode which is buried in the ground.

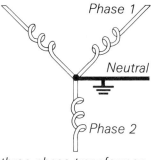

Phase 1

Neutral

Phase 2

A three-phase transformer used in a substation

Between any two phases there will be a voltage present which is equal to the sum of the voltage at each of the phases. Between any phase and neutral there is a voltage equal to the mains (local) supply. In the UK, these voltages are 415 volts between phases, and 240 volts between any phase and neutral

(USA equivalents 208:120). The three-phase and neutral supply is then separated down to feed houses and so on. One phase might feed a road of houses and the next phase might feed another road. If large supply requirements are needed, such as for heavy industry or for theaters, the three-phase and neutral systems can be fed directly into one building and the apparatus within can be split across the phases. The Theatre Royal, in Bristol, England, has an 800 amp per phase, three-phase and neutral supply. This is necessary as there is a dimmer capability alone of 510 kw (equal to 2140 amps).

Earthing (ground)

At the consumer end of the electricity supply, exposed metal parts of apparatus, and also the water and gas pipes, are wired to the ground via another earth electrode. This ensures that should a fault occur in the apparatus or wiring, electricity can travel through the electrode back to the earth at the substation. It will immediately cause a dead short and blow the fuse protecting the apparatus. This makes sure that the faulty equipment is disconnected from the supply for obvious safety reasons.

Fuses

A fuse is simply a weak link in an electrical circuit — a piece of wire that will heat up and melt, should excess current pass through it. A fuse is designed to melt before the rest of the circuit is damaged. The current at which this occurs is known as its rating.

Every phase (live) wire or conductor in an electrical installation must be protected against excess current by a fuse. The rating of this fuse should not exceed the lowest rated conductor in the circuit being protected. What this means, in simple terms, is that to protect a piece of cable rated at 10 amps, a 10 amp fuse must be inserted between the cable and the supply, and so on.

Fuses must always be inserted in the live side of a circuit, as should any switch, because the live wire is the potentially dangerous one. It can give an electric shock or start a fire, if a fault should occur.

When replacing any blown fuse, the replacement must be of the same voltage, current rating, and type as the original fuse (see also page 154). Then it will continue to provide the same measure of excess current protection.

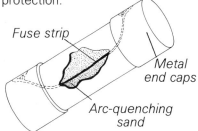

Fuse strip

Metal end caps

Arc-quenching sand

Cut-away of a fuse

Safety

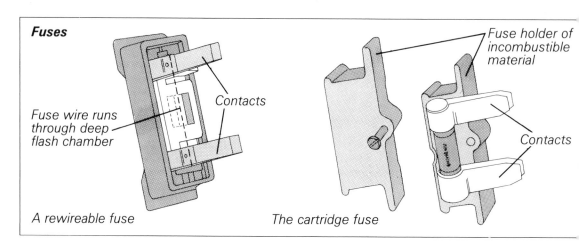

Fuses

Fuse wire runs through deep flash chamber

Contacts

A rewireable fuse

Fuse holder of incombustible material

Contacts

The cartridge fuse

Cables

When replacing any blown fuse, the replacement must be of the same voltage, current rating, and type as the original fuse (see page 153). Then it will continue to provide exactly the same measure of excess-current protection.

Most of the cables that are used in a theater by the lighting crew or department will be for only temporary lighting installations that will last just for the duration of the show concerned.

Therefore the cables will be constantly mobile and must be very durable and flexible, in order to take the strain.

They must be of an approved type for safety reasons and of the correct gauge to carry the necessary current.

Stranded wire, which is made up of small wires grouped together to form a single conductor, is the most flexible and therefore the best to use. Solid wire is normally used only for permanent installations.

Small voltage twin-core cable is very useful for the wiring up of telephone bells, alarms, or perhaps a front-door buzzer.

All cables should be regularly checked and serviced. Always keep an eye open for any crack in the insulation, which could well make the cable potentially dangerous.

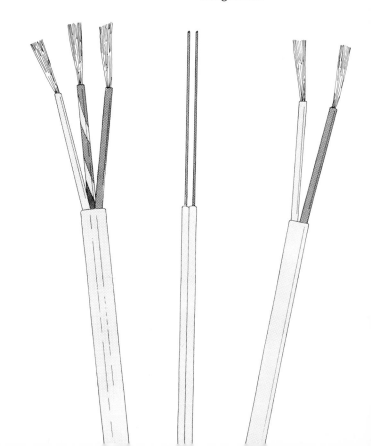

Circuit breakers

A circuit breaker is a current-sensitive switch which will "trip" with any current overload, but which can be reset afterwards.

It's extremely unwise to repair a fuse that has blown (or a breaker which has tripped) without first finding out why this has happened. It is quite likely that the fault still exists. For example, if a short circuit has occurred between the two conductors of a flexible cord, then their insulation may have melted. The conductors will therefore be exposed to touch and could cause a shock if the fuse is replaced.

The fault should be repaired immediately, or the apparatus temporarily disconnected for repair, before replacing the fuse that has blown.

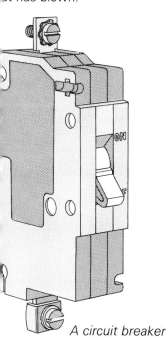

A circuit breaker

Calculating current

It is very important to know how to calculate the amount of current a device uses. This knowledge is important for two main reasons:

1 So that you can be sure that the electricity supply is capable of feeding the device with the required power.

2 So that you ensure that the cable feeding the device is able to take the necessary load.

As theater lighting rigs tend to be temporary, many link cables are used to connect luminaires to their dimmers. These cables must not carry more than their recommended load, otherwise overheating could easily occur. This could result in either a fuse blowing or, worse still, a fire breaking out. ◇

The first thing to do is to find out what size cable is being used. Then check its current-carrying capabilities. (This can be taken from the IEE Regulations in the UK and from the National Electric Code article — which is part of the National Fire Code — in the USA.)

Finally, the luminaire loading for each cable can be calculated, by using the formula below:

$$I \text{ (current in amps)} = \frac{\text{watts}}{\text{volts}}$$

For example, with a 1000 watt luminaire on a 120 volt supply, the luminaire would require a current of just over 8 amps; as shown in the formula below:

$$I = \frac{1000 \text{ (watts)}}{120 \text{ (volts)}} = 8.3 \text{ amps}$$

Thus, the cable used to feed power safely to the 1000 watt luminaire would need a capacity of about 9 amps.

How many luminaires?

The formula used above can be used to calculate the number of luminaires that may be fed from a mains supply of known capacity. If the mains supply is, for instance, 120 volts at 60 amps, the following is true:

mains capacity in watts
= 120 x 60
= 7200 watts

Thus it can be seen that a maximum of seven 1000 watt luminaires may be safely supplied.

Safety ◇

Always electrically isolate any electrical device when attending to it.

Do not plug a luminaire into a hot (live) circuit.

Do not switch dimmers on or off unless all luminaires are faded to "Off".

Do not allow beverages near the control boards, dimmers, or patch panels.

Only a qualified electrician should connect a portable dimming system to the electrical service.

Keep luminaires away from draperies etc.

Check all color frames are securely inserted.

Series and parallel wiring

Series

In series wiring, the total current passes through every appliance in the circuit.

If one lamp or appliance is used in the circuit, its voltage must match that of the supply. By placing another lamp of the same rating in series with the first, the voltage is equally divided between the two, (as shown in the second diagram).

Each 110 volt lamp is now only half as bright as it would be if it were the only lamp in the circuit. This is because it now receives only half its rated voltage.

For the two lamps in series to run at the correct brightness, they would need to have a voltage rating of 55 volts.

In this way, it is possible to use low-voltage lamps on a mains circuit. The voltage rating of the lamp must be divided into the mains-supply voltage in order to determine the number of lamps to use. This is how most sets of Christmas-tree lights are wired.

The drawback with this method is that only one lamp needs to "blow" and the entire set of lamps is put out of action.

Finding the faulty lamp can be quite a long process, especially if there are a large number within the circuit.

Parallel

With a parallel wiring system, the total current is divided between several appliances (fixtures) individually connected across the supply.

The voltage of each appliance must be equal to that of the supply. However, if one lamp in this circuit should fail, the others will not be affected. This is how electricity is normally distributed from the power station to domestic appliances

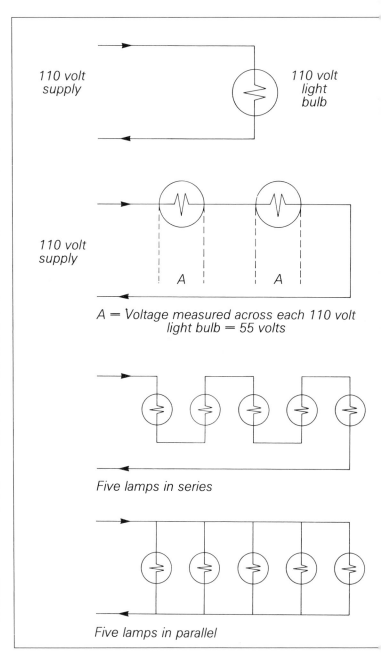

A = Voltage measured across each 110 volt light bulb = 55 volts

Five lamps in series

Five lamps in parallel

ansformers

insformers are the devices
ed to change one alternating
rrent voltage to another. They
nsist of an iron core around
nich there are two windings.
ie winding might have, for
tance, 2000 turns and the
ier, 1000 turns. If the 2000
n winding (the primary
nding) is connected to an AC
pply, then a voltage will
o be generated on the 1000

turn winding (the secondary
winding). This voltage will be
half of the voltage connected to
the primary winding.

The output voltage of the
transformer will depend upon
the ratio of the number of turns
in each winding.

In the example, the voltage was
stepped down, but by reversing
the turns ratio, the voltage can
be stepped up instead.

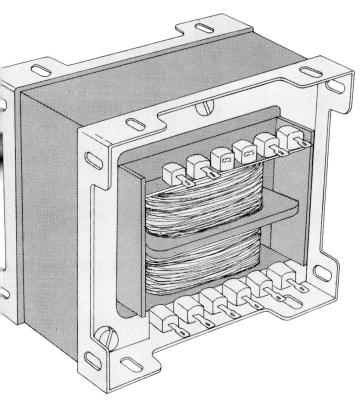

transformer

Precautions

It is essential when carrying out
any electrical maintenance or
wiring to remember at all times
that a potentially lethal form of
energy is being used. However,
if the work is undertaken with a
sense of responsibility and the
correct materials are used, then
a safe repair or installation will
be successfully achieved.

The safety of all electrical
appliances and wiring can be
ensured in three ways:

1 Insulation

Phase terminals or any other
equipment should always be
covered in such a way that no-
one can touch any live parts.

2 Earthing (ground)

Metal casings, or any exposed
metal of an appliance, should be
electrically connected to earth
(ground) to ensure safe use.

3 Protection against fire risk

Always use cable that can carry
the required current loading.
Protect the circuits with the
correct sizes and types of fuses
or circuit breakers.

If the principles in this chapter
are always carefully observed
and the lighting equipment is
regularly checked, then you,
and the theater you are working
in, should remain intact. It is
beyond the scope of this book to
explore the subject in greater
detail but there are many other
books available on electrical
theory and practice. When
working in this field, ignorance
is not bliss!

Lighting productions by John A. Williams

Lighting designers can only successfully develop their art by applying all their ideas in a practical, theater situation. The professional, as well as the amateur, is learning all the time, forever gaining knowledge with experience.

The accumulation of skills is a gradual process but this chapter of the book allows us to tap the knowledge of the expert, as it explores some of the problems and interesting productions that John A. Williams has met in his role as a lighting designer, overseeing a hundred and twenty productions, to date.

We learn just how particular difficulties of some productions were overcome; the way the lighting was approached; and how equipment and techniques can be applied to highlight creatively the special qualities of each piece of theater.

Four plays come under scrutiny: *A Midsummer Night's Dream, The Recruiting Officer, When the Wind Blows,* and *Oh What a Lovely War!*

In each case, the complexities of the lighting can be easily understood and are particularly relevant to the theories already explored in the book.

These productions are all quite different. Not only are the plays dissimilar but the style of production and staging take quite different forms, so many varying lighting techniques a demonstrated. It is hoped th even the larger rigs can appreciated and will be of he even to the beginner. (Far mo complex lighting designs a demonstrated in other boo but have no place within t context of the *"Create Yo Own..."* series.)

It is particularly interesting note that the stimulation trying to solve the spec complications of each p seems to bring the greate satisfaction and success. T resolving of problems "in t field" is the best experien available. Through this chap we see just how this is done

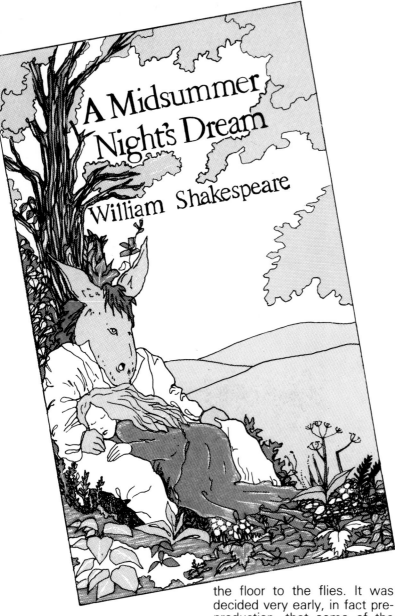

A Midsummer
Night's Dream

William Shakespeare

Richard Cottrell's production of *A Midsummer Night's Dream* at the Bristol Old Vic presented the production team with several technically demanding requirements.

The set design, conceived by Bob Crowley, incorporated a wrap-around cyclorama which enveloped three sides of the staging area all the way from the floor to the flies. It was decided very early, in fact pre-production, that some of the sequences the director had in mind would work only with the use of low cross light — a light that would travel from one side of the stage to the other, illuminating the actors and nothing else.

The most obvious problem was the one presented by the wrap-around cyclorama. This structure, in its initial shape and form, would have prevent any type of masked, low cro light. Together, the set desigr and lighting designer overcar the problem by "tenting" t cyclorama.

When this method is used, t bottom section of the "cy (cyclorama) is actually split several places, in a line from t stage to about the midway pc of the cyc's drop (in t particular case, at about fc meters from the stage floor)

Then, if the upstage edge of t "tent" is pulled off stage and t downstage edge is pulled stage, a hidden space is creat between these two edg where a boom of light can successfully masked.

This method of incorporat cross-light positions in seemingly impossible situat worked very well. Apart fron slight billowing effect, t audience really had no mean: detecting that the cyclora had been split in this way.

The second major task was transform the "cyc" area fron very deep-blue night color daylight. As the majority of t play takes place at night, t prime use of the cyclorama v to create the illusion of the va deep sky at this mystical tin

We decided that, rather th use a white cyclorama and th light it deep-blue, we would ι a royal-blue cyclorama. T problem with lighting a wh cyclorama to create the blue s at night is that the cyclora will "glow" blue, and we neec instead to give an impress of great "depth". Also, wh lighting is used in this way ds to pick up stray and lected light from the stage. ving procured a deep-blue clorama, the only remaining ficulty now was finding a way turn this deep-blue night sky o the color of daylight when uired. It is a simple matter to it color into a sheet of white iterial but far more difficult to ht it out". As it happened, it d already been planned to

use a second surround in front of the cyclorama, so it was decided to utilize this medium to overcome the problem. This second surround was a wrap-around, wide-mesh gauze, which followed the line of the cyclorama. It ran a meter or so away from the upstage section of the cyclorama and then closed up to lie just a few inches away from it down the sides.

On to this wide-mesh gauze were attached hundreds of calico leaves. For the majority of the time these leaves would remain unlit and be simply silhouetted against the blue cyclorama. The floods were placed between the cyclorama and the gauze. (The gauze was drawn away from the top of the cyclorama down the side of the stage to allow for this.)

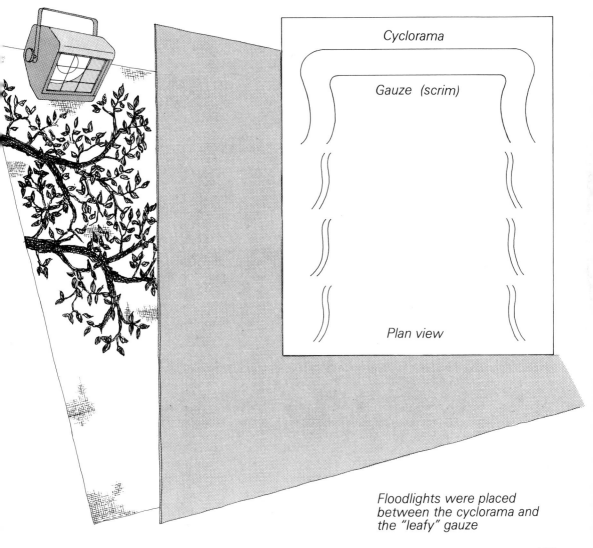

Cyclorama

Gauze (scrim)

Plan view

Floodlights were placed between the cyclorama and the "leafy" gauze

161

A Midsummer Night's Dream

The idea was that, as daylight dawned, the leaves would be lit in a progression of colors until full daylight was reached, and the dark-blue cyclorama beyond quite forgotten. It worked "like a dream"!

The third problem was to find a means of accomplishing the director's vision of the opening sequence in the woods. The technical difficulties were, in fact, two-fold.

First it was decided that the wood should be revealed as moving spangles of light through trees.

Secondly, Puck was then to appear, in a stylized way, dancing around on the upstage portion of the set.

To settle the first requirement, a cheap "moving light through trees" effect was needed. This was achieved by the use of three projectors which were fitted with metal slides of leaf cut-outs. Placed in front of the projectors was a continuously rotating color wheel. This had been fitted not with color, but with metal strips fixed into the color holes.

A smoke effect was billowed into the woods to create an eerie mist. Then the broken rays of light from the projectors with the leaf slides imitated the dance of light through trees.

The rotating color wheel in front of the projectors motivated the individual lines of light, so that they produced a constantly changing effect.

The second problem imposed by the opening scene was how

to light Puck, who was up stage, in an "interesting or unusual manner" (director's quote).

Unfortunately cross light was impracticable — because the "tenting" did not start until farther down the stage.

Front light was considered too boring, and top or back light would not really reveal the character sufficiently to the audience.

So it would appear that bottom light was the only answer. Fortunately the acting area had been designed as a rake, a raised area of stage which sloped to the normal stage level at the sides and front.

It was therefore possible to conceal luminaires in the up-stage portion of the rake. Puck could then stand over each of the luminaires in turn, to be lit in an "interesting and unusual manner", and at the same time, his appearance would be such that the audience would instantly recognize him.

Having discovered ways around the specific problems raised by this production, general decisions now had to be taken.

So much of the stage was being used at any one time, I chose to light the production in what might be termed as area lighting (both from the front, side, and back) with a good number of "specials" thrown in.

The area-lighting rig used was symmetrical, that is to say, the equipment allocation could be seen as a mirror image each side of the center line, although all the colors chosen were

not necessarily symmetric placed. The stage was divi into a grid of twelve sectio and lit as shown on the righ

Each section was front lit, to near a 45 degree convention the theater would allow. F lights were focused into ea area. Two warm colors, number 3 from stage right, a number 73 from stage I and two cool colors (a num 61 on each side).

The overall light was made u full by three colors rigged each side — a medium-gra blue (a number 45 from sta right and a number 40 fr stage left), a golden amb straw (a number 98 on ea side) and a light blue (a num 69 on each side).

There was also a wash apricot (number 47) and a ba light wash of deep blue (num 119), used mainly just to co the stage, as the sculptur was left to the cross light.

The lighting for the whole sta area was very controlla within each section. So muck that one section could be li a relatively "normal" manr while another section could lit in a stylized manner, by us a cross light.

Thus, each section was able take on a different individ quality, and yet, quite import for this production, could a appear to be exactly the sai as another, when necessary

This form of area lighting is always favored, but it can w very well with open staging a was certainly most success on this occasion.

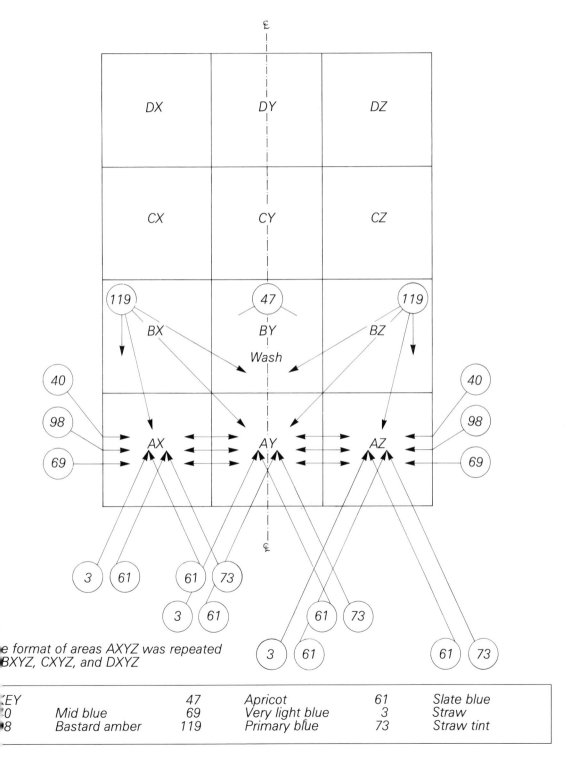

The format of areas AXYZ was repeated
BXYZ, CXYZ, and DXYZ

KEY					
0	Mid blue	47	Apricot	61	Slate blue
8	Bastard amber	69	Very light blue	3	Straw
		119	Primary blue	73	Straw tint

Lighting plan

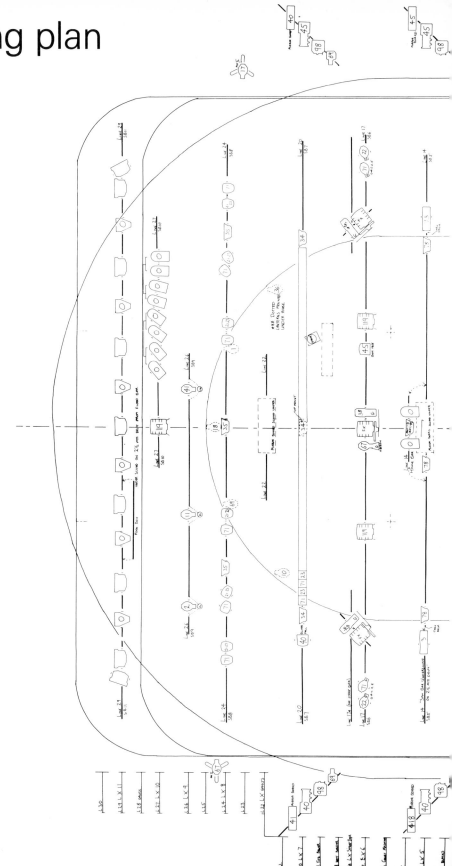

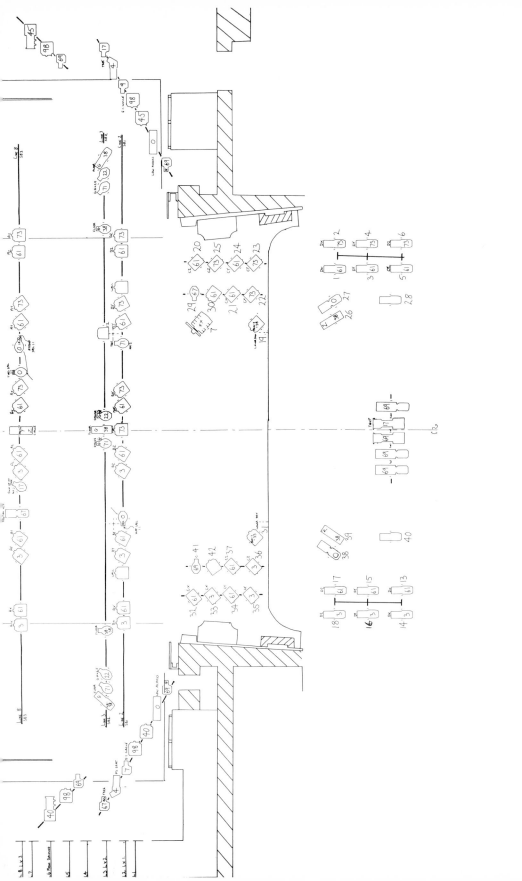

165

Adrian Noble's production of *The Recruiting Officer* was first performed at the Opera House in Buxton and subsequently at the Theatre Royal in Bristol, England. However, it is the production at the Assembly Hall in Edinburgh, Scotland, for the 1979 Edinburgh Festival, which is the most interesting one to examine from the lighting point of view.

To all intents and purposes, the play was lit in the round (or arena). Moreover, the show was also running concurrently with *Troilus and Cressida*, another Bristol Old Vic production. As these two plays were part of a repertoire, the two lighting rigs had to be successfully "married".

Another designer, Francis Reid, was in charge of the lighting for *Troilus and Cressida* so it was necessary for the two designers to co-operate on the project.

Together we designed a rig of such versatility that the only change necessary between the two shows was the switch of colors on eight Par blazers. This simplicity was vitally important as there was very little time available between the two plays — so refocusing or repatching had to be avoided at all costs.

Before proceeding with an explanation of the rig, a description of the set will be helpful. Although both plays used more or less the same

acting areas, the upsta[ge] sections of each were, to s[ay] the least, incompatible.

Troilus and Cressida had [a] drawbridge-type of stairca[se] leading up to an upper lev[el] This staircase was sandwich[ed] between two towers. For *[The] Recruiting Officer*, the [set] designer, Bob Crawley, used [a] sky-cloth, which was inclin[ed] over the acting area at [an] angle of about 25 degre[es] thus effectively masking t[he] staircase and towers.

The principle acting area [of] both plays was a raked sta[ge] measuring 6.5 meters by [?] meters, with the audience [on] three sides. It was decided [to] use a nine-segment format

; three up and three across.
[n]ormal" two-color wash was
[req]uired (one warm and one
[coo]l) and, if possible, it was
[want]ed to light each section from
[all] four sides (that is at 90
[deg]rees separation).

[An]y Fresnels could have been
[use]d here, as sharp-edge
[foc]using on the acting area was
[not] required. Unfortunately, a
[qui]ck calculation revealed that
[the]re would not be enough
[equ]ipment to light each section
[by t]his method — at any rate, no
[uni]ts would be left over for
[spe]cials and other remaining
[req]uirements: so "Plan Two"
[wen]t into operation.

[As] previously described in this
[boo]k (see pages 87-89), there
[are] basically two ways of
[ligh]ting an acting area in the
[rou]nd or a thrust stage. Either
[fou]r lamps can be used at 90
[deg]rees; or three lamps at
[120] degrees (doubling this if a
[two]-color wash is needed).
[Obv]iously, the first method
[giv]es a smoother, finished
[eff]ect. It is also easier to use the
[uni]ts and to "pair" them. The
[sec]ond method is, however,
[qui]te adequate. Both designers
[felt] that the central areas in both
[row]s (CY and BY) were
[defi]nitely strong focus areas. It
[wa]s therefore decided that
[the]se areas would be lit by 90
[deg]rees separation and that the
[per]imeter areas (AX, AY, AZ,
[BX,] BZ, CX, and CZ) would be lit
[by]120 degrees separation.

[An]other unusual problem raised
[by] the design was that the
[cen]ter part of the acting area
[(CY] and BY) was wider than the
[per]imeter areas. So the area CY
[wa]s lit by the format shown in
[dia]gram 1.

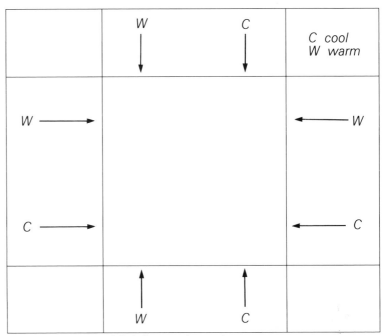

1 Ideal method of lighting each section

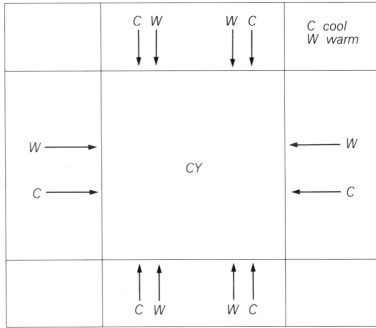

2 Possible method of lighting a wider area

The Recruiting Officer

Because lights could not be rigged directly behind area BY, the format shown in diagram 3 was used for this section:

The other perimeter sections were lit by the rather more conventional method, using 120 degree separation.

To allow flexibility of control, each angle had its own dimmer. The lighting of the basic nine areas needed thirty dimmers and, with the doubling up required by the two-color wash, the overall plan demanded sixty dimmers and channels. The final arrangement, shown in diagramatic form, is on the opposite page (diagram 5).

Having decided on the area cover, a mutual choice of color was needed for the area wash. The cool wash was no problem. Both designers wanted a fairly substantial blue because, as well as cooling the lighting states, there were some long night scenes to be catered for. Therefore Cinemoid 61 (slate blue) was mutually acceptable.

However, the color for the warm wash was slightly more difficult to arrange. Most of the "warm" states in *The Recruiting Officer* were to be exteriors. Therefore it would obviously be preferable if pinks could be avoided, and colors from the straw range chosen, such as straw (number 3), straw tint (number 73), or no-color straw (Rosco 804). Perhaps even open-white would work?

Troilus and Cressida, on the other hand, included a large number of interior states, and a set that, on occasion, would benefit from some pink toning.

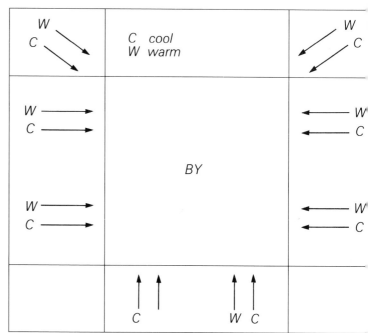

3 *This section could be lit from the front and sides only*

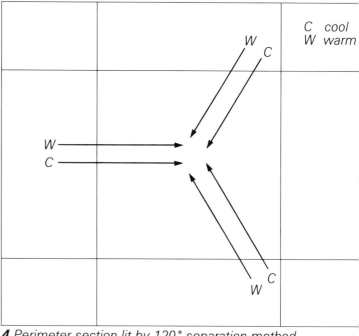

4 *Perimeter section lit by 120° separation method*

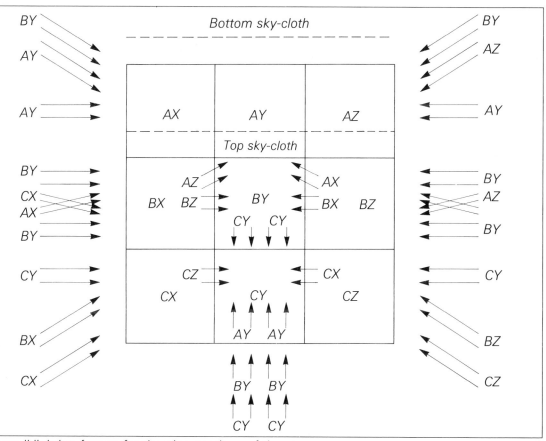

BY

AY

AY — AX — AY — AZ

Bottom sky-cloth

Top sky-cloth

AZ AX
BX BZ — BY — BX BZ
CY CY

BY
CX
AX
BY

CY

BX

CX

CZ — CX
CX CY CZ
AY AY

BY BY
CY CY

BY
AZ
AY

BY
AZ
BY

CY

BZ
CZ

Overall lighting format for the nine sections of the stage

ne "pros and cons" of all the nts in the pink and straw range ere discussed at length. /entually, it was decided that a raw would be the most utually beneficial color wash, oviding that it was not too eep a tint. So a "no-color-raw" (Rosco 804) was the final ompromise. Pink toning was otained for *Troilus and ressida* by adding some pink ownlight wash (number 52).

ne sky-cloth for *The Recruiting fficer* was lit with ten 1 kw ear T/H (tungsten/halogen) ods. Five 252 projectors

provided clouds, stars, a rainbow, and forked lightning. Because of the angle of the sky-cloth, the projectors had to be dropped 1.5 meters from the main lighting grid to lessen distortion; and, as seen from the plan, they had to be sited at the far end of the rig to prevent shadows being created by the other luminaires.

Each show, of course, used its own specials, which were occasionally borrowed by the other production. For example, there were sixteen Patt 23s with "break-up" gobos, which

were used to texture the upper set on *Troilus and Cressida*. Used at a low level, these gobo effects were also very helpful in *The Recruiting Officer*, when they served to relieve the monotony of the plain sky-cloth.

Thus the limitations imposed by the in-the-round staging and the sharing of the lighting rig were all overcome successfully and, in fact, utilized to very good effect. Working within quite strict disciplines can actually fire the creative spirit — so do not be daunted by a seemingly impossible situation.

169

Lighting plan

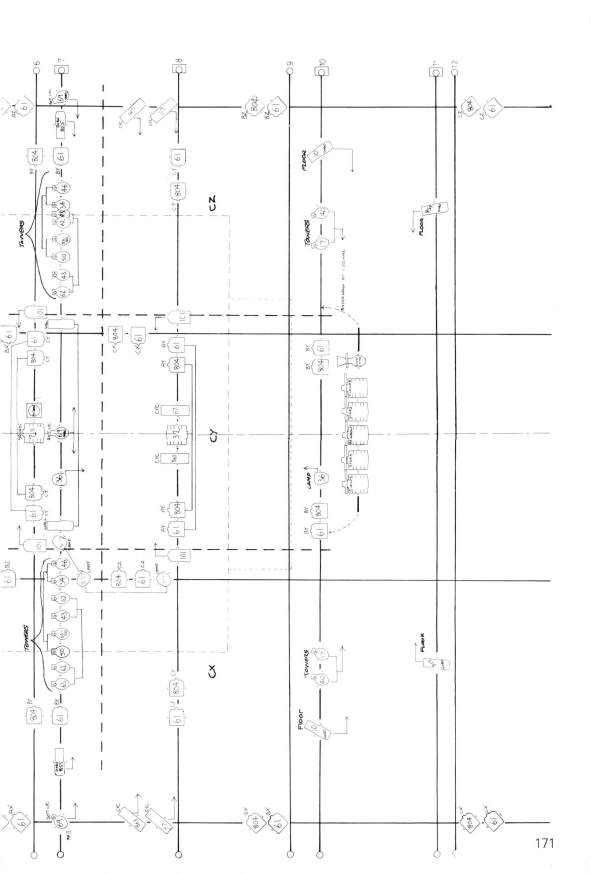

171

WHEN THE WIND BLOWS

Illustration © Raymond Briggs

When the Wind Blows was one of the most evocative theatrical pieces it has ever been my experience to light. It was also one of the most exciting, claiming much critical acclaim for its special effects when it opened in the West End. Credit for these effec must be shared with Dav Bryant (production electricia and Nick Jones (soun designer). A brief descriptio of the play's content may he to illustrate the spec problems involved in lightin this production.

The play is focused on th experience of two of the mo famous characters created the author, Raymond Brigg These are Gentleman Jim a his wife, Hilda, who live in idyllic little home in t country. Here they fa together the horrors of nuclear attack and t subsequent after-effects.

During the holocaust th receive no immediate injurie except minor burns but, as th play progresses, they slow die from the effects radiation. Hilda's naïve throughout their plig underlines the sheer terror such an event.

The broad outline of t lighting requirements w planned so that it would follo and amplify the degradation life after the explosion.

Therefore it would begin with bright and sunny, cheer summer's afternoon. T designer, Billy Meal, ha created a simple but ve effective set. This featured bungalow on stage with, as were, the front wall remove

A path led around th bungalow and also enclosed small front garden. cyclorama encircled the se with a tree and a telegra pole set in front.

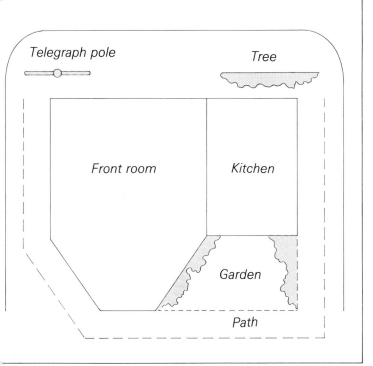

Telegraph pole

Tree

Front room

Kitchen

Garden

Path

an of the set

irly strict area separation was
quired. Each of several "units"
eded to be lit in its own right,
to be combined with others to
ake an overall picture with no
rd lines. These units within
e set were the front room, the
chen, the garden, the path,
d the foreground.

e creation of the nuclear
plosion itself presented the
eatest challenge of all. This
as to be far more than a
nple "off-stage" noise. It was
tually to be seen on stage.
e target area was assumed to
some distance away and the
ngalow several miles from
e actual center of the blast.
erefore a few quite different
fects would need to be
eated. These were as follows.

1 A blinding white flash

2 A shock or pressure wave
(accompanied by sound effects
and the semi-destruction of the
bungalow on stage)

3 Heat blast and wind

4 Revelation of the aftermath

To try and create a "visible"
nuclear explosion on stage,
even the effect away from the
epicenter, was a new and very
exciting undertaking for all
those concerned.

In the event, the elements
actually used were all readily
available. Nothing brand-new or
previously unknown was made
or invented. Nevertheless, the

scene required a good many
hours of work to fit the various
effects together and to time
their co-ordination correctly.
(This applied particularly to the
lasers.) Only then would the
illusion work.

The two fundamental elements
the lighting department had to
deal with were the blinding
flash and the heat haze. Also,
after the explosion, the lighting
had then to reveal the sudden
desecration of the home.

First of all, the problem of how
to create the nuclear flash was
discussed. The director, David
Neilson, wanted the flash effect
to light the stage with such
brilliance that the audience
would be momentarily blinded.
To achieve this with reflected
light would be incredibly
difficult. All the pre-production
experiments with 5 kilowatt and
10 kilowatt luminaires proved
this to be true. However, turning
the lamps to face the audience
did not really work either,
because the filaments required
such a long time to cool down.

At last, after much discussion
and experimenting with various
effects, a final decision was
reached. The light source would
have the greatest impact if it
faced the audience. So the
filament problem would simply
have to be overcome by some
means. Lighting units were
therefore required which could
heat up and cool down
extremely quickly, rather like a
strobe. The unit eventually
chosen was a Jupiter Six. Each
unit contained six Pars.(These
were FCX : 120 volt, 650 watt.)
Their quick response was just
as required and the blinding
effect suitably dramatic.

173

When the Wind Blows

The set before the nuclear explosion

The heat haze was the second special effect required. It was hoped that this would be a fairly long and progressive effect, lasting for about twenty-five seconds. We had already decided that the white flash should be directed towards the audience, so it was thought that the heat haze should also be pointed in their direction. Somehow we needed to create a swirling wave of heat which would spread above the audience. After considering all the possibilities, it seemed that using a laser was probably the only answer. This decision immediately created two more fresh problems:

In the first place, the cost, and second, how to satisfy the health and safety department that any danger had been eliminated. As it happened, both problems were quite eas overcome. This was becaus we elected to use four low-cos 0.5 milliwatt neon lasers, whic were no bigger than a kitche roll tube. They did not sc mechanically, so no spec operator would be require Moreover, these lasers we low enough in power to t considered within a catego where safety regulations we readily accomodated. The uni

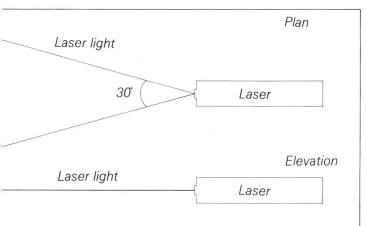

Plan

Laser light

30°

Laser

Elevation

Laser light

Laser

:h laser gun produced an effective "fan" of laser light

nned optically (by beaming
laser through a lens at the
d of the laser gun) to create a
degree "fan" of laser light.

cause neon lasers were
ng used, the color of the light
s red — perfect for our
eds! To see laser beams (or
light beam), a medium is
uired. After all, fresh air does
"light up". It is only the dust
ticles present in the air which
ch and reflect the light so as
nake the beam visible to our
es. Smoke was therefore
oduced to enhance the
ect. It is in the nature of
oke to swirl and drift in laser
t so this gave a very good
pression of fierce heat. The
cing of the lasers was crucial.
achieve the very best effect,
light should be aimed

towards the audience, rather
than coming in from behind
them. The lasers would also
need to be placed as low as
possible, so that the audience
could actually look along the
length of the beam towards the
laser gun. To achieve this ideal
position, the laser guns would
have to be placed on the stage
(hopefully the direction in which
the audience would be looking!)

Because of their small size, it
was no problem to hide the
laser guns discreetly. All that
remained was to ensure that,
should they drop on their axis,
there could be a means of
cutting off the lasers' light
before it reached audience eye
height. To meet this stipulation,
a very simple box construction
around the gun was required.

Further to this, it may be worth
mentioning that lasers can, of
course, create some stunning
effects, and that really there is
nothing that can simulate their
rather special characteristics.
Used sensibly and with care,
they are perfectly safe.

High-powered lasers, because
they are potentially dangerous if
incorrectly handled, can be
used only with the assistance
of an experienced operator.
Current health and safety
regulations ensure this. There
are, however, categories of
laser that anyone can buy or
use, provided that certain
guidelines are adhered to
carefully. A copy of the code of
practice regarding laser use is
available from any local Health
and Safety department (or the
Food and Drug Administration in
the USA).

One slight disadvantage of
using lasers is that they can only
be switched on or off; so the
effect may look rather abrupt. In
order to avoid this unnaturally
sudden appearance, it was
decided to try and find a way of
somehow "introducing" the
lasers. To this end, a red "light
curtain" was placed across
the top of the proscenium arch
from which the lasers' light
would appear.

A light curtain is a straight row of
lights, usually Pars, each of
which gives as parallel a beam
as can be contrived! The overall
effect is a strong curtain of light.
The greater the inclination of the
lights' angle to the audience,
the greater the effect of the
curtain. A good light curtain
will "mask" anything behind it,
providing that the area behind
remains unlit.

Laser light

Light cut off here
should the unit drop

Laser

x construction around the laser gun

When the Wind Blows

To give the right effect, the light curtain could, of course, be gradually brought up to full intensity. Once again smoke was required. This time it was used to obtain the best effect from the light curtain. Once lit, the laser light emerged from behind this curtain of light.

The wind effect was created by four wind machines, which were placed behind the proscenium and then masked by the light curtain as they were flown into position.

As the dust and debris cleared, the set was to be slowly revealed, starting first with a silhouette of the house, and then showing the broken telegraph pole and the tree now stripped of its leaves. This was achieved simply, by lighting the cyclorama and nothing else.

The sequence of events:

Black-out
Blinding light
Sound effect: house shakes and is then devastated:
Smoke on
Light curtain on
Lasers on
Wind machines on
Wind machines off
Lasers off
Light curtain fades out
Silhouette
Complete lighting state

It may be of interest to know that the sound was not used merely to create an audible effect, but also had a dramatic physical effect. Such was the force of the sound effect, that the chandeliers, and the theater itself, literally shook. Everybody there experienced a thumping sensation on the chest.

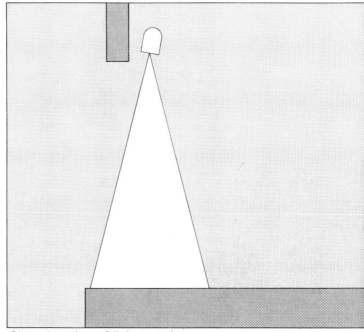

Side elevation of light curtain

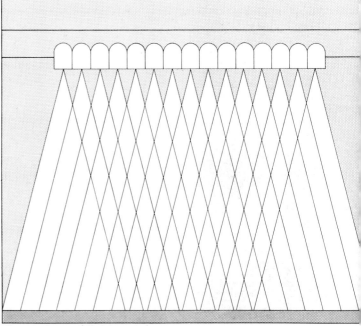

Front view of light curtain

e impression of the set being stroyed on stage, despite its being actually visible, was nvincing because of all the shing and banging, and cause of the swirling heat ce that dominated everything d looked very eerie. Most of destruction of the set was complished by using electro- chanical means.

The lighting of the set was based on very strict area separation, so that it was all easily controlled. The overall effect was of a shock to all the senses, which none of the audience would care to repeat in real life.

This combination of especially dramatic effects was made

possible only by the co- operation of all the different production departments. As often happens, their particular areas of responsibility tended to overlap each other. In this instance, the mix of effects occupied just a few moments of stage time and so the impact was especially powerful.

e aftermath of the nuclear explosion

Lighting plan

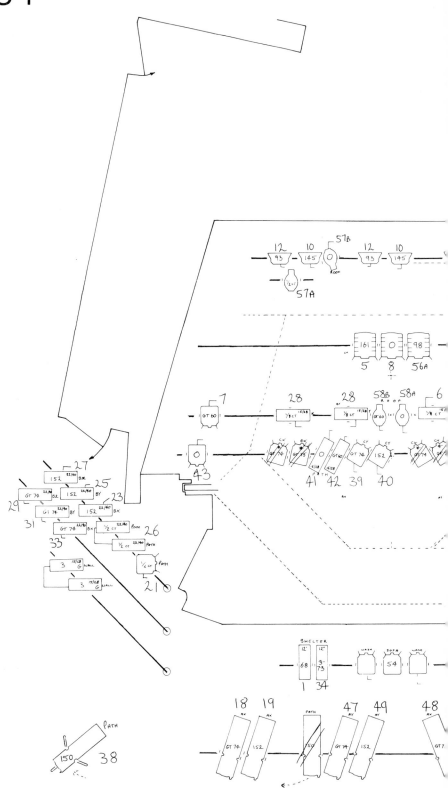

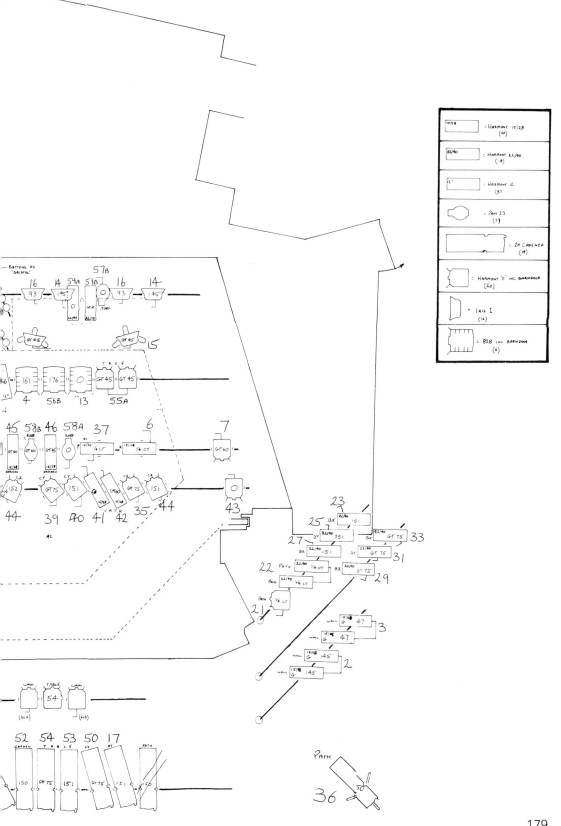

Bristol Old Vic Trust Limited gratefully acknowledges financial assistance from the Arts Council of Great Britain, the City of Bristol and the County of Avone

Lighting a musical

When lighting a musical, principles remain the same for any other production. Th is no need to have sleeple nights worrying about complexity of the lighting. true that there may be m more lighting states and c than are normally required with careful pre-planning, need not be such a daun prospect. In fact it is a g opportunity for the light designer to explore avenues, to enjoy the excuse use color more lavishly t usual, and also to experim with a few special effects.

However, the fact that production is a musical does imply that the work can undertaken without discipl Far more is involved than sim rigging lots of colored lights using a few follow spots. Or again, every luminaire will pre-planned and must be gi a specific job to do. Fol spots, in particular, may requ extra rehearsal time, so as establish and practise cues.

Oh What a Lovely War! is interesting production to stu not only because it is a musi but also as the staging at Bristol Old Vic involved a squ rig, and so was rather unus

The set used was, in fact, v simple. It consisted of jus scaffold cube with two scaff towers at either side. On e corner of the cube were batt of red, white, and blue b that "chased" (flashed off on in sequence). The sid front, and back of the cube w used to hang luminaires, t creating a square rig.

is square rig was by no means purely decorative. The nt bar was used to frontlight e upstage area, the side bars give a wash of side light, and back bar was rigged for back it. Black masking flats were ced down the sides of the ge, thus allowing booms to hidden behind them. On to se booms were rigged ninaires for side light and low cross light. The rest of the rig was constructed as shown on the plan at the end of this section (see pages 184-85).

It is important when lighting a musical to remember that some moments in the show may be played "straight". That is to say, there will be no music, no brash color, and no follow spots. So it is always advisable to provide a good area cover, as previously described. The stage area used in this production was such that a division of twelve sections was needed (three across and four up). This was then all marked up and lit in the normal way — except for the D area, which was used so little that only two luminaires were used for each area (one in a warm color and one in a cool).

DX	DY	DZ
CX	CY	CZ
BX	BY	BZ
AX	AY	AZ

The stage area for this production was divided into these twelve sections

Oh What a Lovely War !

The colors chosen for these front lights were normal tints (S1 Gold tint and 40 Pale blue). The same colors were used in both sides of the rig. The sculpting quality was achieved by the level difference — which meant no pairing of these luminaires was necessary. The whole area was backlit in open white for "normal" conditions.

When lighting a musical, it is a good idea to have a few really strong colored washes ready, in case there is a suitable moment in which to use them. A backlight structure is best used to avoid lighting the actors' faces with strong color. The colors for *Oh What a Lovely War!* were green, blue, and red (38, 63/20, 64).

There were certain moments in the show when the director required splashes of color, rather than a heavy wash. This was achieved by a spot bar of pattern 23's (500 watt profiles) fitted with break-up gobos. Each profile was given a different color and focused to cover all the staging area.

Under normal conditions, the image from 500 watt profiles (fitted with gobos and with moderately heavy color) would be "washed out" by the main rig lighting the actors. However, as follow spots were being used to light the actors and singers during these moments, the problem did not apply. It should be noted that quite subtle effects can be achieved by using follow spots to light actors or singers. This is sometimes a welcome relief from the powerful and bright, or highly colored lighting states so often associated with musicals.

Musicals usually contain a good deal of dance. The most flattering way of lighting body form is from the side. To shape and sculpture the dancer is often more important than highlighting the eyes and faces. In this way "lighting the dancers so they can be seen" needs a different approach. Use a good strong side light for the dance sequences and do not flatten it by adding too much front light.

Indeed, when lighting the scene at the plotting session, build the state by introducing the side light first, adding as little front light as possible if needed.

In the case of *Oh What a Lovely War!*, the side light came from three booms and one perch on each side. Further side light came from the upstage and downstage bars on stage. Their purpose was to sidelight the "normal" scenes in the play.

A five-color wash was used from the side; one straw, two blues, one pink and one white. These were set low on the boom. The first luminaire was only about half a meter from the stage floor. (Lights that are rigged this low are sometimes referred to as "shin-busters"!)

The decision to use profiles on the bottom two luminaires was taken in order that these could be shuttered off the stage floor. Because they were so low, the resulting booms would go from one side of the stage to the other, lighting just the dancers and singers without lighting the floor. This meant that gobo patterning could be used on the stage floor without being washed out by any of the stage illumination.

As can be seen from the plan at the end of this section, quite a number of specials were needed in order to light specific moments in the show.

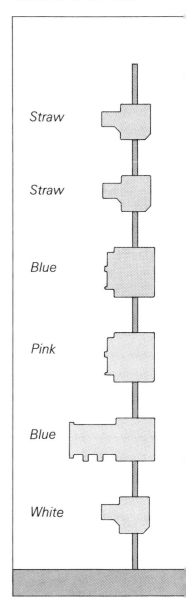

Straw

Straw

Blue

Pink

Blue

White

Typical construction of a boom used in the show, with general color description

de projection was also used ectively in the show. The een was dropped in and out position as it was required. cause the screen was not permanent fixture, no back ojection was possible. Back ojection is usually preferred, a brighter image can be nieved with this than with nt projection. Moreover, with ulti-slide projection, there is vays a possibility of a slide coming jammed. If the ojector is on stage, it may be ssible for the stage manager a stage electrician to be able free it. However, if the ojector is in a remote position the front of house area, then jammed slide could spell aster. So, when there is a oice, do elect for back ojection if possible.

e careful cueing of a musical absolutely vital if the lighting signer is to achieve a creative erpretation of the show. Very en the light cues are linked to change of rhythm, a certain at, or a specific dance move.

It is certainly a time when it is essential to work very closely with the stage manager or whoever will be "on the book" (cueing the show). Certainly one should spend rather more time in rehearsals than one would for a conventional play.

Taping the musical numbers can be very useful. Usually everything happens so quickly in a musical that it is impossible to take notes and watch the stage at the same time. Taping the show enables the lighting designer to plan the cues and changes in a more relaxed and efficient way.

Thus it can be seen that lighting a musical requires the same basic techniques as any other production. The role and aims of the lighting designer should remain unchanged.

In order to achieve these aims, however, the actual choice of lighting structures may differ. More side light, especially, may be used than is normal in a conventional play; as well as top or back light. Bolder, more lavish color effects may also be appropriate.

There is also the possibility of experimenting with more unusual special effects to add to the visual impact of a dance or song. Throughout, methodical pre-planning of all the cues and lighting states will be essential.

Lighting plan

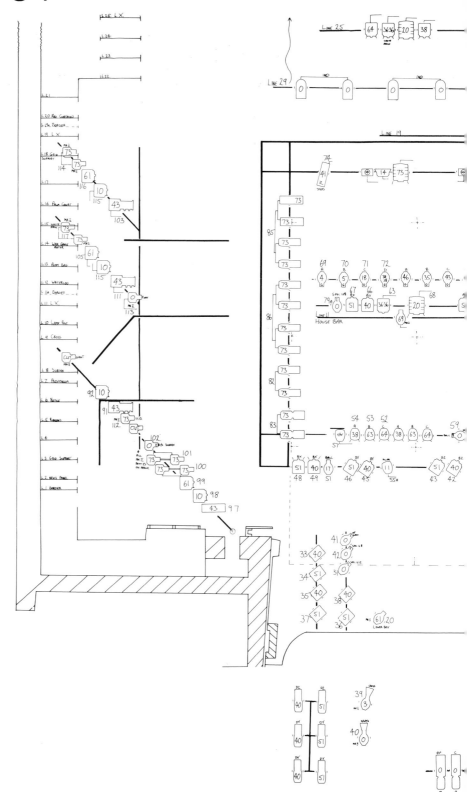

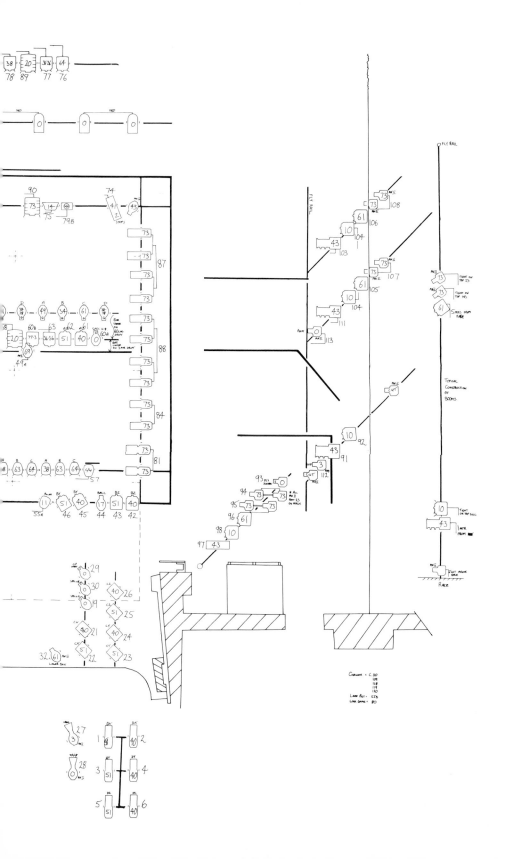

185

Glossary

Acting area The area of the stage upon which the actors will perform; area separation

Adapter or splitter A means by which two or more electrical devices can be made to share the same power point

Ampere A measurement of the rate of flow, or current, of an electrical circuit

Area separation Dividing the acting area of the stage into suitable units that can be lit independently or together

Auditorium The audience area beyond the stage

Backcloth A scenic canvas or "drop" used across the back of the stage, often serving as a sky-cloth

Bar Pipe or barrel above the stage for the suspension of lighting and scenery; may be called a batten

Barn doors Four separately hinged doors on a pivoted frame at the front of Fresnels or P C's. These can be used to shape the beam and prevent spill light

Batten Bar from which lighting equipment can hang: also applied to compartment-type lighting or border-lights

Blanket color Overall wash of unrelieved color of exactly the same tint

Boom or light tree A vertical pipe which can support several luminaires on a number of boom arms

Bosun's (or boatswain's) chair A wooden seat slung on a rope which is used when working aloft

Chasing lights Lights that flash on and off quickly in succession

Cinemoid Cellulose acetate which is used to make color filters in the UK

Color correction A means by which colors can be adjusted to give the desired effect; for instance, special filters may be needed to achieve a more acceptable white

Color magazine A color boomerang, a device which holds color media and enables quick changes to be made to the color of a follow spot etc.

Composite gel Different colored pieces of color gel cut to fit together into one color frame

Counterweight system Method by which apparatus can be loaded on to a flying bar and be safely balanced by weights in a cradle

Cross-fade To fade or change from one lighting state to another

Cross plugging A system whereby several luminaires can be made to share the same circuit or dimmer alternately or at different times

Cue When appertaining to lighting, this indicates the moment at which a lighting change will be initiated. The cue may be a line in the play, a change of tempo in a song, or a particular piece of action on stage — whatever has been entered on the cue sheet

Cue count The time it w take, in seconds, to execute lighting cue

Cue sheet A chart on whi all the lighting cues of production are recorded a which the board operator electrician will use

Cyclorama or sky-cloth curved or straight backclo hung at the rear of the stage is sometimes painted white a then lit as required

Derig The removal of t lighting rig at the end of production

Dimmer A device whi regulates the power in t circuit feeding a lamp, so as alter the intensity of the light

Diorama A scenic view representation made with partly translucent painting. If t light shining through it is varie then the effects change

Dry ice Frozen carbon dioxi which can be used to produ mist or steam effects

Earthing Means by which, f safety reasons, metal parts electrical equipment may wired to the ground

Fill light Light which fills t shadows the key light create

Fit-up The rigging of t lighting equipment prior to production

Flare Usually refers to lighti spill, or can be spectral-fla rainbow effects

Flat or peak field T distribution of light intens

186

ross a beam), which can be
enly spread or concentrated
one area (peak field)

es The area above the stage
ere scenery and lighting
uipment can be suspended
: of sight or "flown"

bats or footlights A
ten of lights set at the front of
: stage, which in historical
es consisted of floating
wicks

ods Floodlights giving a
de beam of light, sometimes
psoidal reflectors

cusing In theatrical
minology, this does not
cessarily mean achieving a
rp focus. Instead it
scribes organization of the
ection, position, shape, and
er of the beam — as directed
the lighting plan by the
ting designer

ont of house (FOH)
hting positioned in the
ditorium which is directed
vards the stage

te Aperture between the
it source and the lens on a
file spotlight; may have
lt-in shutters with which the
am can be shaped, as well as
ners which allow for the
ertion of an iris or gobo

uze or scrim Large-
eave cloth used for scenic
ects which can be rendered
her transparent or opaque
cording to the direction and
ensity of the lighting

latine A color filter
edium, which is made of
mal gelatin; it is rarely used
wadays

Gobo (or cookie) Template
of thin metal with cutout design
or pattern which can be
projected; normally used with
profile spotlights

Ground plan Scale drawing
of a set as seen from above

Ground-row lighting Strip
light lighting scenery from
below; lengths of shallow
lighting equipment or battens,
for low-level lighting effects

Hire company A rental
company

House bar A permanent
flying line

Irises These can be inserted
into profile spotlights to vary the
size of the beam

Key light A light of high
intensity, or the most dominant
direction of light; the most
important light on a set which
focuses attention, such as
moonlight through a window

Lamps The high-power
electric light bulbs used in
theatrical lighting equipment

Legs Unframed scenery,
canvas wings, or curtains which
are hung vertically to mask the
sides of the stage

Lighting bar Lighting or
electrics batten, or pipe

Lighting plan or plot A
scale drawing detailing the
exact location of each luminaire
used in a production and any
other pertinent information

Lighting rehearsal A
rehearsal of the lighting effects
on stage, usually without any

actors, during which any
necessary adjustments can be
made to the luminaires

Lighting state The format of
lighting used at a particular
time; a "lighting picture"

Lighting structures The
different angles of light used in
stage lighting: top light, side
light, front light etc.

Light tree See Boom

Luminaire tails Electrical
pigtails or lantern tail; the ends
of cable attached to a luminaire

Luminaires The instruments,
lanterns, or units used to light
the stage; lighting fixtures

Magazine battens Border
lights or battens which are
"flown" above the stage (UK)

Mains operated British term
meaning electrically powered,
using the "mains" voltage at
local or domestic level

Masking To hide certain parts
of the stage or equipment from
the audience, using scenic
devices

Masque A popular court
entertainment in 16th and 17th
century Europe, performed by
masked players and usually
based on a mythological theme.
It often included music, dance,
and poetry, as well as
spectacular effects

Master A dimmer control (a
fader) which controls other
submasters, which in turn
control the dimmers

Mock-up A structural model
of the stage and set, often a

Glossary

forerunner to the final detailed model, made to scale

Open (or exposed) rig A rig used on an open, unmasked stage without a proscenium arch or borders, so the lighting will be visible and not hidden from the audience in the conventional way

Pairing lamps Joining more than one luminaire to one circuit

Panoramas A painted cloth which can be wound across the stage to reveal a constantly changing view

Patching Using a cross-connect panel which allows any of the stage circuits to use any of the dimmers

Perches Platforms set behind the proscenium arch and used for lighting equipment; luminaires positioned in this area are sometimes called tormentor spots

"Practical" A lighting fixture which is apparently used on the set by the actors during the production, and so is visible to the audience and must be operational. Can also mean any fixture or prop which is illuminated

Preset A group of faders. Can also mean a pre-arranged lighting state being held in readiness for future use

Profile spot Ellipsoidal reflector spotlight; provides a soft or hard-edged beam of light focused by a lens system

Proscenium arch The stage opening which, in a traditional theater, separates the actors

from the audience: sometimes called the "fourth wall"

Pyrotechnics May mean fireworks, but in lighting circles generally refers to any bangs or flashes that might be required!

Raked stage A sloping area of stage which is raised at the back (up stage) end

Rig The lighting construction or arrangement of equipment for a particular production

Roundel Can mean a colored glass filter used on striplights. In the historical section of this book, it refers to a small circular window or niche

Run-through or run
Seeing a performance of a play (or one aspect of it, such as the lighting) all the way through, from beginning to end

SCR Abbreviation for a silicon-controlled rectifier; a solid state semi-conductor device which operates as a high-speed switch and is used in dimmers

Shutters Part of a luminaire which determines the profile of the beam and can be used to prevent lighting spill on the edges of the stage or set

Sightlines Imaginary lines drawn from the eyes of the audience to the stage, to determine the limits of stage which will be visible from the auditorium

Specials Any light which is used for a special purpose or isolated moment in a production rather than being used for general area lighting

Spill light Unwanted li[ght] which spills over its requi[red] margins or shows through a g[ ]

Spot bar Batten or pipe which spotlights are hung

Stage cloth or drop vertical area of painted can[vas] which can be a backcloth, fr[ ] cloth, or drop cloth, depend[ing] on its position on the stage

Submaster This controls [a] number of faders in a gr[oup] master control system, and i[s in] turn controlled by the mas[ter] dimmer on the consul

Tabs Stage curtains acr[oss] proscenium arch

Tallescope A scaffoldi[ng] mobile tower which enab[les] electricians to rig the lumina[ire] at a height of up to thirty-six f[eet]

Temperature The warmt[h] coolness of lighting colors

Throw distance Distan[ce] between a luminaire and [the] area on the stage that it will li[ght]

Thrust stage A stage wh[ich] is surrounded by the audie[nce] on three sides

Tormentors Masking fl[ats] angled up stage and set at [the] edge of the proscenium

Tripe (bundle) Bunch [of] cables bound into single stra[nd]

Tripe ends or pigtail Sh[ort] cable that protrudes from [a] connecting strip or drop [box] (US) at the end of a stage circ[uit]

Volt A unit measurement [of] electrical pressure betwe[en] two points in a single circuit

Index

Bibliography and Acknowledgements

Bellman, Willard F.
Lighting the Stage; Art and Practice
Crowell 1974

Bentham, Frederick
Art of Stage Lighting
Pitman House Ltd 1980

Bergman, Gosta M.
Lighting in the Theater
Rowman and Littlefield 1977

Gillette, J. Michael
Designing with Light
Mayfield Publishing Company 1978

Hughs, G.J.
Electricity and Buildings
Peregrinus 1984

McCandless, Stanley
A Method of Lighting the Stage
Theater Arts Books 1958

McPartland, J.F.
Handbook of Practical Electrical Design
McGraw-Hill 1984

Morris, Noel M.
Electrical Circuits and Systems
Macmillan 1980

It is also important to read the **National Electric Code (USA) And the IEE Regulations (UK)**

Palmer, Richard H.
The Lighting Art: The Aesthetics of Stage Lighting Design
Prentice-Hall Inc. 1985

Parker, W. Oren & Smith, Harvey K.
Scene Design and Stage Lighting
Holt, Rinehart & Winston Inc. 1979

Pilbrow, Richard
Stage Lighting
Cassell Ltd 1979

Reid, Francis
Stage Lighting Handbook
Pitman 1982
A & C Black 1982

Rosenthal, Jean & Wertenbaeker, Lael
The Magic of Light
Little Brown & Co. 1972

Sellman, Hunton D. & Lessley, Merrill
Essentials of Stage Lighting
Prentice-Hall Inc. 1982

Thompson, Francis G.
Electrical Installation and Workshop Technology
Longman 1984

Warfel, William B.
Handbook of Stage Lighting Graphics
Drama Book Specialists Publishers 1974

Rank Strand Limited
PO Box 51, Great West Road,
Brentford, Middlesex, TW8 9HR
United Kingdom
CCT Theatre Lighting Limited
Windsor House, 26 Willow Lane,
Mitcham, Surrey, CR4 4NA United Kingdom
Theatre Projects Covent Garden Limited
10-16 Mercer Street, London, WC2H 9QE
United Kingdom
Meltdown Limited
57-59 Long Acre, London, WC2E 9JZ
United Kingdom

Raymond Biggs
Illustrator and author of *When the Wind Blow*
and the publishers:
Hamish Hamilton
Garden House 57-59 Long Acre, London.
WC2E 9JZ United Kingdom
Bristol Old Vic Trust Limited
Theatre Royal, King Street, Bristol, BS1 4ED
United Kingdom
Mike and Tim Evans (Small beginnings)
John Elvery (Notes on projection)
G. John Davies B.Sc., C.Eng., MIEE
(Consultant engineer)